Community in Tweedsmuir Camp, Surrey after WWII

Commemorative Edition

Zen Rogalski
Wies Rogalski

Old Kiln Museum Trust

**Tweedsmuir Camp
Exhibition**

Sections of this booklet were first published in 2003 and 2007

Updated and revised in 2012 for the launch of the *Tweedsmuir Camp Exhibition* at the Rural Life Centre

www.TweedsmuirMilitaryCamp.Co.Uk
www.TweedsmuirCampExhibition.Co.Uk

Published by the Old Kiln Museum Trust

© Zen Rogalski and Wies Rogalski

Funded by the Heritage Lottery Fund

All rights reserved. Apart from any use permitted under UK copyright law, no part of this publication may be reproduced or transmitted in any form or by any means, electronic or mechanical, including photocopying and recording, or held within any information storage and retrieval system, without permission in writing from the publishers or under licence from the Copyright Licensing Agency. Further details for such licences may be obtained from the Copyright Licensing Agency Limited, Saffron House, 6 to 10 Kirby Street London EC 1N 8TS

ISBN 978-0-9573865-0-1

Cover Design: Zen Rogalski

Printed by Blackmore Ltd.
www.blackmore.co.uk

Dedication

To both the Canadian soldiers who built and passed through Tweedsmuir Camp during the Second World War and the Polish families who lived there between 1947 and early 1960

Contents

vi   Map showing routes of Polish civilians and Polish Forces 1939 to 1945

vii   Map showing Locations of Polish Airforce, Army and Navy in the British Isles - June/July 1940. (The Polish Government in Exile was based at The Rubens at the Palace, Buckingham Palace Road, London)

viii   Acknowledgements

ix   Introduction

12	Chapter 1	Origins of Tweedsmuir Camp
22	Chapter 2	Lorne Scots (Peel, Dufferin and HaltonRegiment)
30	Chapter 3	Participation of Poland in World War Two and the consequences of the Yalta Conference
40	Chapter 4	Transfer from the Polish Armed Forces to the Polish Resettlement Corps: an unarmed British unit
48	Chapter 5	Families, dependants and orphans
52	Chapter 6	The Origins of Tweedsmuir Camp as a place for Resettlement
60	Chapter 7	Family life and Domesticity

68	Chapter 8	Patterns of Employment
76	Chapter 9	Cultural Life
82	Chapter 10	Schooling and Children
92	Chapter 11	Demise of Tweedsmuir Camp
102	Chapter 12	After Tweedsmuir Camp
112	Chapter 13	Personal Stories and Individual Achievements
136	Chapter 14	Final Comments
152	Chapter 15	Saturday morning Polish School at Milford, including children's work
178	Image Credits	

The coloured photographs at the start of each chapter heading are used to illustrate the appearance of Tweedsmuir Camp as it was between the years 2000 and 2010, and to encapsulate how the site has changed since the camp was first constructed in 1941

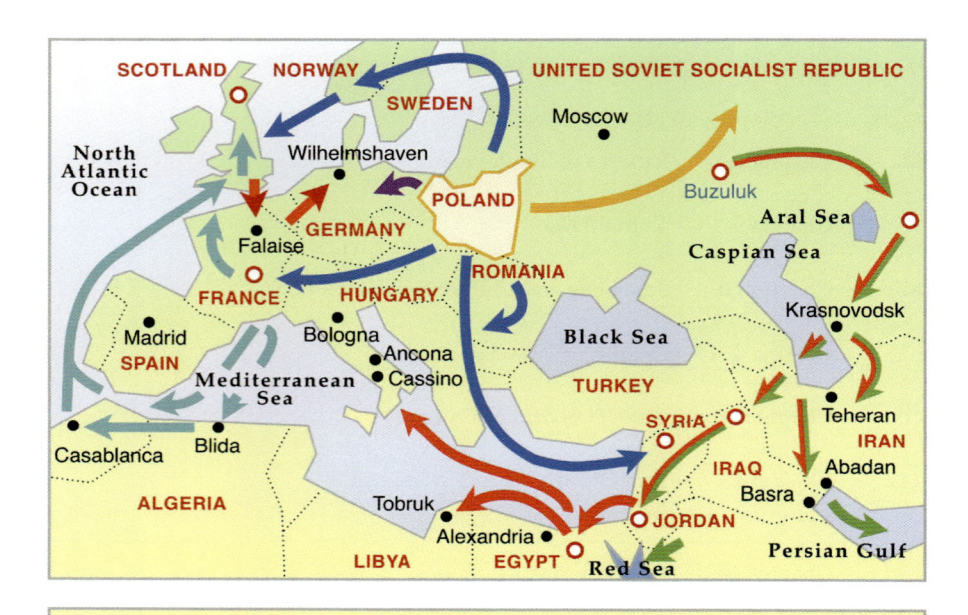

Legend:

- Withdrawal of Polish Forces after the fall of Poland **(1939)**
- Deportation of civilians and Prisoners of War to Nazi Germany **(1939-1940)**
- Withdrawal of Polish Forces after the fall of France **(1940)**
- Deportation of civilians and Prisoners of War to the USSR **(1940-1941)**
- Movement of Polish troops to theatres of war **(1940-1945)**
- Evacuation of civilians and the newly formed Polish Army from USSR **(1942)**
- Evacuation of civilians to safe havens such as India and Rhodesia **(1942-1943)**
- O Locations at which Polish troops were required to muster

Routes of Polish civilians and Polish Forces 1939 - 1945

Legend

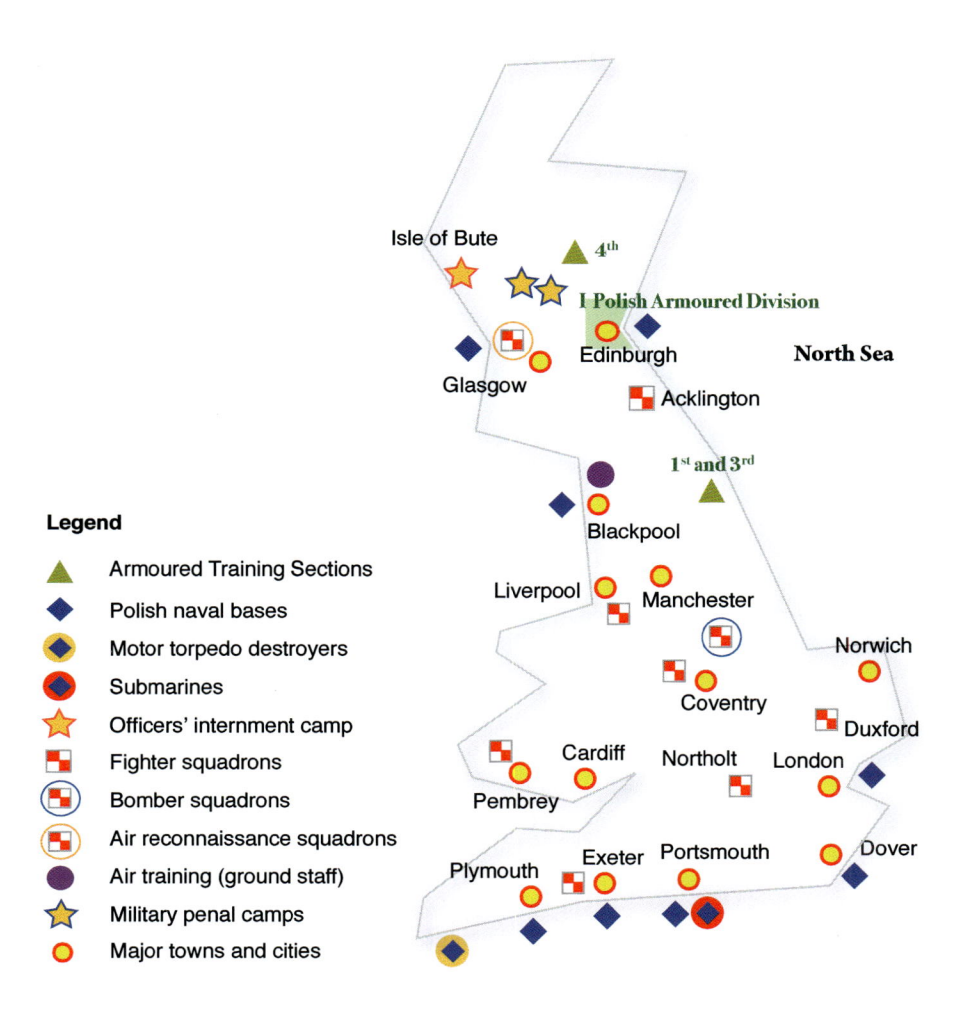

- ▲ Armoured Training Sections
- ◆ Polish naval bases
- ◆ Motor torpedo destroyers
- ● Submarines
- ★ Officers' internment camp
- ▦ Fighter squadrons
- ▣ Bomber squadrons
- ▣ Air reconnaissance squadrons
- ● Air training (ground staff)
- ★ Military penal camps
- ● Major towns and cities

Locations of Polish Airforce, Army and Navy in the British Isles June/July 1940

Acknowledgements

A large number of children and adults have contributed to the contents of this publication. We greatly appreciate their contributions and endeavours.

Before writing this booklet, we had to complete research at the National Archives, and at the Polish Institute and Sikorski Museum (PISM). Dr Andrzej Suchcitz, Keeper of the Archives at the PISM, has been particularly helpful in guiding our investigations and analyses; his understanding of the history discussed in this booklet is second to none.

Similarly, Chris Shepherd, Director of the Rural Life Centre, Surrey, should be mentioned for providing guidance and advice concerning the content of the exhibition and this booklet. His unconditional support is greatly appreciated.

We have also had to rely on the professional guidance of David Fairhead in the production of the DVD, which complements the booklet and augments the exhibition. His rare talent has enabled us to produce a film that brings to life some of the areas covered in this publication. John Collins, a film-maker at the BBC, should also be cited as he shot all the scenes, giving up his time unreservedly.

We should like to record our appreciation for the work completed by the children at the Saturday morning Polish School at Milford. Their tasks are reproduced in the last chapter of this publication. Equally, the children's teachers and parents should be applauded for encouraging them in their endeavours. We should like to mention in particular the Director of the Polish school, Dr Zofia Łuklińska, and one of the parents, Marek Plaskota, both of whom coordinated the assignments.

We should also like to thank Charles Allenby for taking the time to read the finished manuscript before publishing.

Introduction

The content of this booklet has been designed to complement the *Tweedsmuir Camp Exhibition* at the Rural Life Centre (RLC) in Tilford, Surrey, England. It is a complex history of Polish people who found it impossible to go back to Poland after World War Two due to their apprehension at returning to a communist led country. While writing, we were conscious of the fact that visitors to the exhibition may be unfamiliar with this history. We should like to think, however, that our endeavours within these pages will at least go part of the way to explain why around 70 families settled, after World War Two, in a quiet corner of Surrey close to Thursley village.

We start by exploring the nature of the land upon which Tweedsmuir Camp was first erected in 1941 and why it was built there. During World War Two the camp was administered by the Lorne Scots (Peel, Dufferin and Halton Regiment), a Canadian Army unit. Although we shall illustrate the Lorne Scots' tenure at Tweedsmuir, it is the Polish community that we shall bring into sharp focus by concentrating on issues such as culture, work, schooling and family life. In so doing we shall use the noun "community" to identify a cluster of people who gelled into one group that worked together.

When the Polish people first arrived at Tweedsmuir Camp in 1947 they were a completely random collection of individuals, comprising adults and adolescent children who were born in Poland. Their language was Polish, the children's education was interrupted by war, and in some cases the fathers, or heads of families, had died during the war. By 1950 couples newly married in the United Kingdom started their own families. Thus, for the next decade, Tweedsmuir Camp accommodated a mixture of people: the older generation and adolescents who were born in Poland, and the younger, recently married people with their own children born in Britain. In some cases the newly married couples comprised a Polish head of family and an English wife.

Just how successfully the Tweedsmuir Polish community, with its own culture and traditions, integrated into British society is a question that is also addressed in this booklet. However, it is a subject that may be addressed on so many levels, such as economic, social, individual and group, and psychological integration. It is also a subject that may be tackled within the context of at least three generations: those who first settled in Tweedsmuir in 1947 to 1948, their children and their grandchildren. The process of integrating such a group into a British way of life had varying degrees of success. We will endeavour to show why as well as some of the resulting consequences for the Tweedsmuir Polish community.

By the time Tweedsmuir Camp was closed it had boasted a strong community with its own social structures and hierarchy. Two issues have permeated our thinking about this project. Firstly, the point at which this group of people became a community, and secondly the factors that influenced its formation. These matters will be clarified in the subsequent pages of this publication.

It was never the intention for the camp to remain a permanent fixture. Therefore, we shall also consider what happened to some of the people from this community after Tweedsmuir numbers had started to dwindle around 1956/57, and after the camp ceased to exist in the early part of 1960.

In the text, we have used the noun 'Tweedsmuirian' or its plural 'Tweedsmuirians' to identify the people who either lived at Tweedsmuir Camp immediately after the Second World War or the people whose ancestors had lived there. Each of the nouns is placed in-between inverted commas because they are words that have been conceived for this text. Nevertheless, using them in a combined form, such as *a first generation 'Tweedsmuirian'*, or *second generation 'Tweedsmuirians'*, determines exactly who is being discussed without the need of any further explanation.

Another word that we should like to bring to the readers' attention is barracks, which we use throughout this text to describe a wooden building, Nissen hut or a group of buildings, in which the Polish population of Tweedsmuir Camp were accommodated. It is common to refer to one such building as a barrack and to two or more buildings of this type as barracks. The word barracks is a *pleural noun*. A 'barracks' is a place where soldiers are billeted, irrespective of whether it is one soldier in one building or one hundred soldiers in fifty buildings. The word 'barrack' as a *verb* has one of two meanings: to house (people, usually military personnel) in a building, or to shout against someone or jeer rudely.

Tweedsmuir Camp was one of many military installations that housed Polish ex- soldiers, their families and dependants after the war. As the history associated with all such camps is similar it should be possible to apply this study to any one of them. There are, however, a small number of exceptions where the camp may have served as a school or a hospital for the newly arrived Polish people. Yet even here, the cultural similarities and traditions would have been easily recognised and understood by any Polish visitor.

This project attempts to uncover a unique social history. It focuses more on the people as individuals, the choices they made in life, and the problems they faced as they endeavoured to achieve success in a foreign country rather than their previous military endeavours. But it will obviously be necessary to provide some military background to this work as without it the social history would be incomplete.

Zen Rogalski, Kent, England
Wies Rogalski, Surrey, England

July 2012

Chapter 1

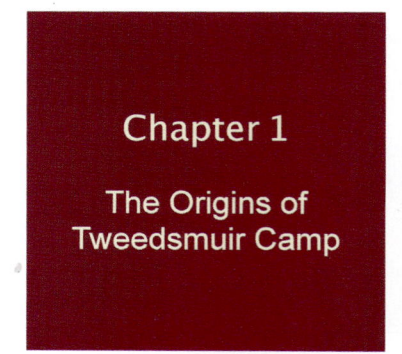

The Origins of Tweedsmuir Camp

• Appearance of the land that lies to the east of the site that was Tweedsmuir Camp

Tweedsmuir Camp was built in 1941 on War Office (later Ministry of Defence) land, which it bought in 1922 - the same year that Sir Winston Churchill purchased Chartwell, his country residence in Kent.

The site of Tweedsmuir Camp lies on the western edge of a valley between Houndown and Thursley Common, 600 metres north east of Thursley village cricket green. The above photograph was taken at the bottom of Thursley cricket green.

Soon after it was bought in 1922 the land upon which Camp Tweedsmuir would be erected became a Summer Camp for British soldiers who were billeted there under canvas for Rest and Recuperation purposes (Fig.1:1). However, in its early history the camp was known as Beansides Camp after a wood located at the highest point on the site (Fig.1:2). Later it was renamed Camp Thursley after the village which lies in close proximity to the site.

Fig.1:1 Appearance of site when it was used by British soldiers in the 1930s as a summer camp

While Fig. 1:2 illustrates the terrain as it was in 1920, the legend below identifies some of the features visible in Fig. 1:1.

The site formed part of the Dye House estate in the 1800s, and was used for rearing sheep. As the ground of the site slopes steeply from west to east, a water management canal was excavated (item 3 on the map) to prevent the lower regions of the site becoming waterlogged and hence unmanageable. The canal is evident on maps dating back to 1871. A stone bridge linked the

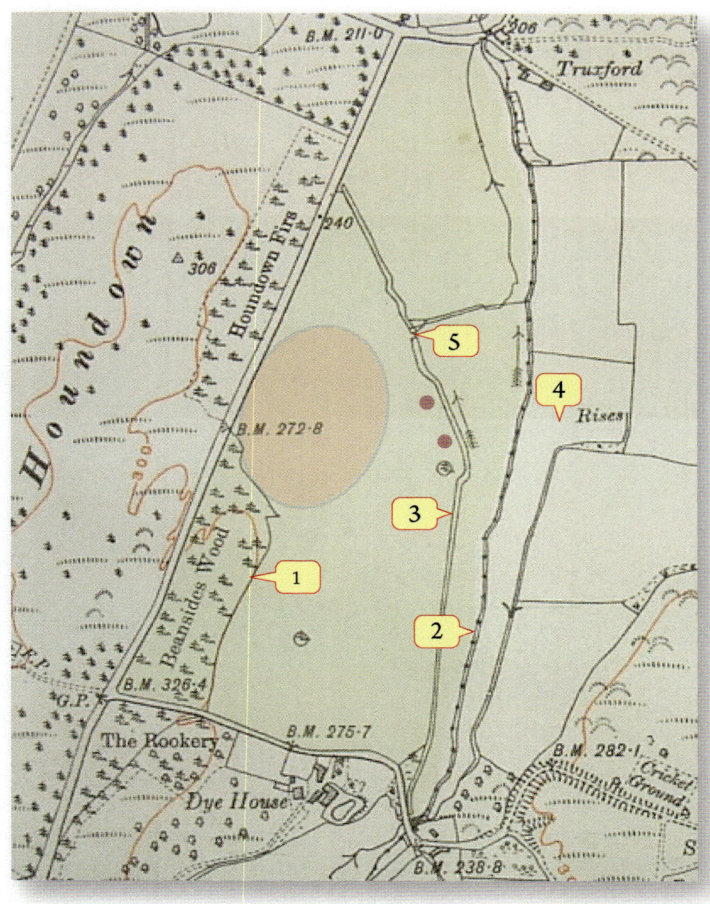

Fig.1:2 Portion of map published in 1920, showing the later site of Tweedsmuir Camp - shaded in green

Legend

Tented accommodation shown in Fig. 1:1

Portion of water management canal as shown in Fig.1:1

1 Beansides Wood
2 Stream
3 Rainwater management canal
4 Approximate position from where the photograph in Fig. 1:1 was taken
5 Stone bridge and sluice gate or weir

13

two areas either side of the canal. When the bridge was first built a farm gate was installed across its deck. What remains of the canal and stone bridge can still be seen today (Fig. 1:3).

Fig.1:3 Remains of canal and stone bridge

The build of Tweedsmuir Camp was authorised by the War Office (WO) on 28 October 1940. The camp's name was changed from Thursley to Tweedsmuir, following Routine Order 761, issued on 6 June 1941. The name 'Tweedsmuir' was chosen by Canadian Military Headquarters (CMHQ) in honour of Lord Tweedsmuir, the 15th Governor General of Canada, who had died on 11 February 1940. He is better known as John Buchan, the author who wrote, among other books, *The Thirty Nine Steps*.

At first the intention was for the camp to be built by a civilian labour force who were contracted to complete the work by 31 May 1941. However, by February it was becoming clear that a shortage of construction workers was resulting in delays. The matter was urgent because over 330,000 troops had recently landed in the UK following their evacuation from the beaches of Dunkirk, and all required accommodation. However, as Canadian officers pointed out, billeting men under canvas was acceptable during the summer but not in the winter months.

After much debate, a resolution was agreed between Canadian and British officers: Britain would pay for the materials to build the camp and Canada would supply the materials by diverting them from builds that were earmarked for Iceland. Lieutenant-General Andrew McNaughton, Commander 1st Canadian Army, UK, argued successfully that the British labour force working on the Tweedsmuir site should be moved to other camp construction sites in the Aldershot Area and be replaced by Royal Canadian Engineers (RCE). They started work on 19 April 1941. It was accepted, however, that in the interest of safety the sewage treatment plant, which was located in the southern most part of the camp, would be constructed by a British civilian workforce because they were familiar with the required statutory regulations.

• Fig.1:4

The management of the RCEs was overseen by a newly created Works Directorate under the command of Colonel Mackenzie, CMHQ. When the camp was completed it included all the characteristics one would expect to see in a military installation such as an outdoor rifle range and an indoor pistol range, a parade ground, a gymnasium, and NAAFI. For recreation there was a cinema and a tennis court, which was erected in 1946 for troops returning from theatres of war.

British firms were often used to supply additional materials for completing the camp's construction. For example, red bricks from *Warnham Brickworks* (Fig. 1:4) in West Sussex and white glazed bricks from the *Leeds Fireclay Company Ltd* (Fig. 1:5) were ordered to complete the sewage plant. An entry in the Works Directorate Diary on 10 July 1941 indicates that 21,000 bricks were

• Fig.1:5

used in the construction of the backstop for the outdoor firing range (Fig. 1:6), and that they were delivered from Hambledon (probably Nutbourne Brickworks Ltd, Vann Lane) over a period of 15 days. Nutbourne Brickworks Ltd was later renamed Nutbourne Works and is now awaiting redevelopment.

Prior to building the camp, the southern section of the site was terraced, or sculptured, to make it more conducive to construction (Section S-S in Fig. 1:7).

• **Fig.1:6**

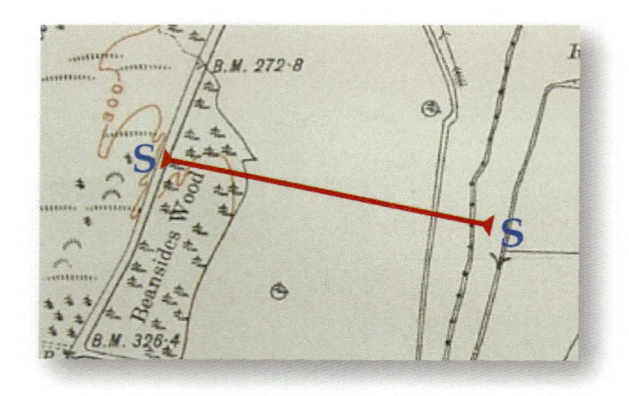

• **Fig.1:7** Section S-S

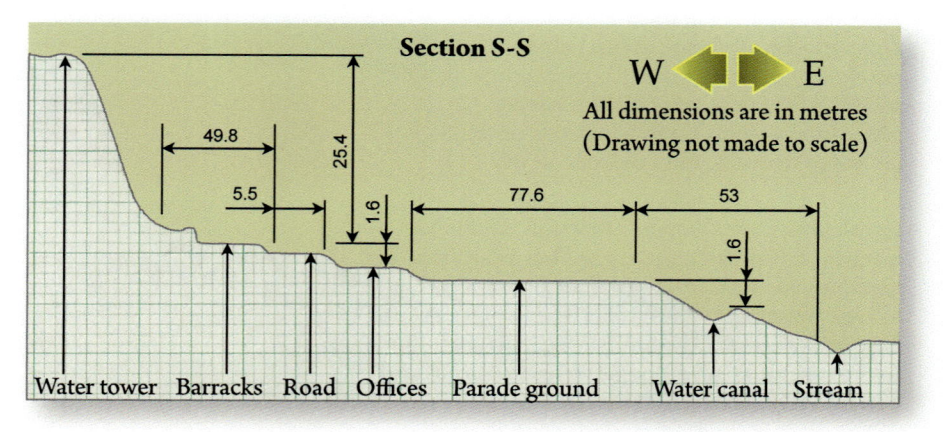

Section S-S

W ⬅ ➡ E

All dimensions are in metres
(Drawing not made to scale)

49.8
25.4
5.5
1.6
77.6
53
1.6

Water tower | Barracks | Road | Offices | Parade ground | Water canal | Stream

16

The terraced landscape, as illustrated by the colour photograph in Fig 1:8, may be seen clearly to the east of the camp's main road. The northern section of the site, as illustrated by the monochrome picture to the right, was left largely untouched during the construction phase of Tweedsmuir Camp.

• Fig.1:8

The parade ground slopes west to east, allowing rainwater to drain from its surface towards a deep gutter which is found along the whole length of the parade ground's eastern border. By making a careful study of the terrain upon which the parade ground was laid, it becomes clear that it is the largest area of flat land on the site, and that its eastern boundary was both raised and terraced deliberately. This raised aspect can be seen at the north eastern corner of the parade ground as shown in Fig. 1:9.

• Fig.1:9

The effort that went into building Tweedsmuir Camp was repeated elsewhere in Britain as the country prepared for war. However, not all

17

the camps were built to the same specifications. In Tweedsmuir Camp, for example, the road system was finished in poured concrete, while the preference in other camps was tar-macadam.

Tweedsmuir Camp's roads included expansion gaps, drainage systems and kerbs (Fig. 1:10): an impressive array of technical features incorporated into the build of a site that was supposed to have been temporary!

Equally, it comes as a surprise that the supposedly temporary nature of Tweedsmuir's construction did not prevent the inclusion of a sewage plant and a water supply system that were thoroughly and carefully conceived. The sewage plant was so efficient that the cleansed water was pure enough to be released into a stream that flows along the eastern border of the camp's remains (Fig. 1.11), at the lowest point of the camp's geography.

Most of Tweedsmuir Camp's western border is 91.44 meters above sea level: an ideal location for a water tower, the inclusion of which was insisted upon at the time of the camp's construction by Mr Teale from the Wey Valley Water Company (now Thames Water). Teale was concerned that the five Canadian camps under construction (two at Bramshott, one at Ludshott, one at Thursley [Tweedsmuir] and one at Headley), would "load to the limit" the company's ability to supply water to the area. A water tower, however, would ease the problem by supplying water to Tweedsmuir Camp

Expansion gap

• Fig.1:10

• Fig.1:11

personnel at peek times without putting a strain on the supply of water. The water tower, under discussion in May 1941 (Fig.1:12), continues to stand in Beansides Wood to this day.

Notwithstanding Teale's concerns, Tweedsmuir Camp's water consumption rose steadily during its occupation by the Canadian military. Recorded meter readings, for example, show that 505,400 gallons were used in the month ending 31 December 1943, rising to 602,000 gallons in the month ending 29 February 1944. These statistics, however, were still just under the predicted rate of consumption.

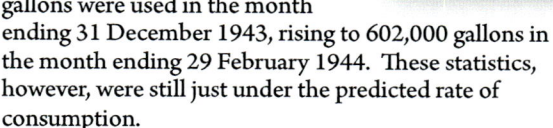

• Fig.1:12

Teale was not the only civilian executive engaged during the camp's construction. The WO employed the services of a Supervising Civil Engineer by the name of Mr Satchwell. He was responsible for controlling the quality of the build. For example, he had to ensure that the right materials were delivered to the site on time, and that buildings were redesigned as and when the need arose. Due to the shortage of steel, for instance, he altered the original plans for the indoor firing range, substituting steel posts with brick columns (Fig. 1:13).

Although by the autumn of 1941 Tweedsmuir Camp was nearing completion, slow progress was being made by the civilian contractors on the installation of the sewage treatment plant. "In an emergency personnel" could have been "housed in the camp, but due to the delay caused by the lack of sanitary and plumbing fittings, bucket latrines" would have had to be used. During November cinder paths were being laid, blackout screens fitted to barracks' windows and other "miscellaneous items" attended to. It wasn't until Wednesday, 26 November 1941 that the barracks in Tweedsmuir Camp were deemed ready for occupation. That afternoon a "Handing-over Board was held" at which point the responsibility for the camp was

• Fig.1:13

passed on from the Works Directorate to the quartermaster at CMHQ who decided the role Tweedsmuir Camp would play during the Second World War.

Clearly this is not a complete account of all construction activities that were undertaken by both the Royal Canadian Engineers and British authorities, but the above does illustrate the nature of the work done under very difficult, war conditions.

Although documentation about the exact cost of building Tweedsmuir Camp has proved elusive, it is possible to deduce an amount, albeit roughly. At about the same time as the camp was being built the RCE were also involved in erecting a Motor Transport Ordnance Depot some 12 kilometres south west of Tweedsmuir, at Bordon, East Hampshire (Fig. 1:14). In a memorandum to Brigadier JH MacQueen, DQMG, written on 24 August 1941, Colonel Mackenzie stated that the total estimated cost for constructing the ordnance depot, based on WO figures and inclusive of materials and labour, was £215,000. At the time of writing the cost of building the same depot today would be close to a staggering £7.5 million! Since the depot at Bordon and Tweedsmuir Camp were of about the same size with similar facilities, it would not be too far off the mark to suggest that both builds were of a similar cost.

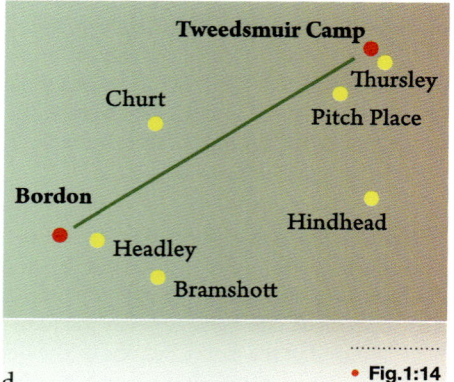

• Fig.1:14

20

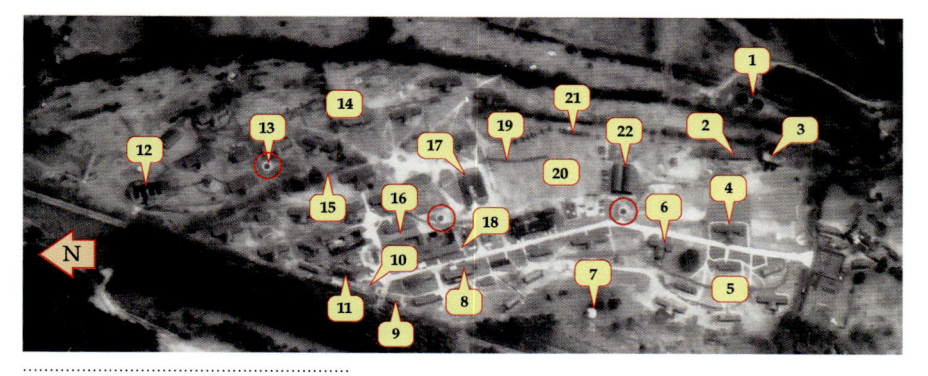

• **Fig.1:15** Tweedsmuir Camp in 1946

Legend for Fig. 1:15

1. Water treatment plant. Access to the plant was provided via an entrance in Dye House Road.
2. Small arms (revolver) range.
3. Rifle range.
4. Officers' Mess with a lawn to the front elevation.
5. Officers' quarters. Located to the south of the camp, away from the other rank's quarters, which were located to the north of the camp (No.14).
6. Sergeants' Mess.
7. Water tower constructed at the highest point in the camp.
8. Orderly Office. It is from here that general daily orders were issued.
9. Kit storage room. This was the original Guard House until 1943.
10. Brick Guard House, which was finished in late October 1943.
11. Motor transport garage. A large corrugated sheet steel structure painted black.
12. Hospital, comprising 4 Nissen huts.
13. Water filter bed, of which there were three (circled in red).
14. Other ranks' quarters.
15. 19th Century stone bridge, spanning a water management canal.
16. NAAFI.
17. Washroom and laundry.
18. Cinema and theatre with stage.
19. Column of soldiers marching off the parade ground.
20. Parade ground.
21. Parked military vehicles.
22. Gymnasium - 2 large Nissen huts constructed next to each other with communal walls removed.

An aerial photograph, measuring 2,440mm x 1,220mm, may be seen at the *Tweedsmuir Camp Exhibition*, Rural Life Centre, Tilford, Surrey.

Chapter 2

Lorne Scots (Peel, Dufferin and Halton Regiment)

Tweedsmuir Camp main road, looking due south. The road was completed in the summer of 1941

Before understanding what life was like for the Polish families who lived at Tweedsmuir Camp it would be appropriate to consider the camp's Canadian phase, which is described briefly on the next eight pages.

The 1 Canadian Infantry Division landed in England on 17 December 1939 with the intention of joining operations with the British Expeditionary Force (BEF) in the summer of 1940. By 23 May, however, it became clear that events on mainland Europe were not going according to plan hence the decision was taken to set aside this blueprint and to launch instead Operation *Dynamo*, dubbed by the British press as the 'Miracle of Dunkirk'. *Dynamo* lasted eight days (28 May to 4 June) and was successful in saving the lives of an Allied Force that numbered 338,000 strong. The safety of Britain now became of paramount importance for two reasons: first to provide a comparatively secure haven for training and holding fighting units and second to plan how best to rescue Europe from the continued tyranny of Nazi Germany. However, placing men being prepared for war under canvass was not an option. Hence, as part of a plan to accommodate the retreating troops, in October 1940 the WO authorised the construction of five 'Yukon' hutted camps at Bramshott North, Bramshott South, Ludshott, Thursley and

Headley, each for about 1,000 men.

During the Second World War Tweedsmuir Camp acted as Number 1 Non-Effective Transit Depot (1 NETD). It was administrated by a detachment of Lorne Scots (Peel, Dufferin and Halton Regiment) under the command of Lieutenant-Colonel Louis Keene (Fig.2:1). His command comprised only men. Keene was a greatly respected officer whose leadership skills were honed during the Great War. He was a cultured leader who had many talents, one of which was art. His paintings were worthy of being exhibited internationally in Canada and in London.

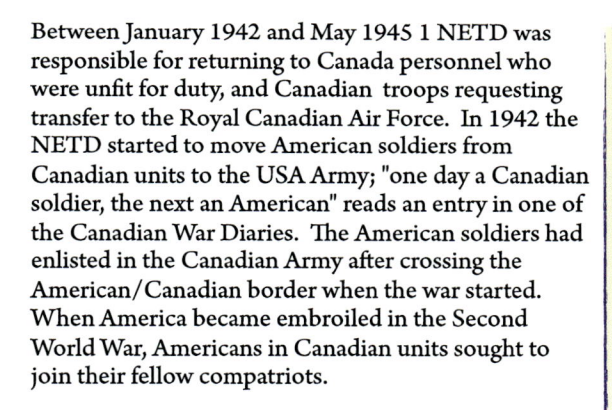

• Fig. 2:1

Between January 1942 and May 1945 1 NETD was responsible for returning to Canada personnel who were unfit for duty, and Canadian troops requesting transfer to the Royal Canadian Air Force. In 1942 the NETD started to move American soldiers from Canadian units to the USA Army; "one day a Canadian soldier, the next an American" reads an entry in one of the Canadian War Diaries. The American soldiers had enlisted in the Canadian Army after crossing the American/Canadian border when the war started. When America became embroiled in the Second World War, Americans in Canadian units sought to join their fellow compatriots.

When the war ended I NETD was renamed Number 1 Canadian Repatriation Depot. Its role now was to repatriate Canadian troops who had fought in mainland Europe. The last Canadian soldier left Tweedsmuir Camp on 21 February 1947, when, in the words of Major (later Colonel) Charles Perry Stacey (Canadian Historical Officer) 1 Canadian Repatriation Depot "ceased to exist." See also (*f*) opposite.

Tweedsmuir was the very last Canadian camp to close in the United Kingdom. After February 1947 only CMHQ at 2 Cockspur Street London, with its magnificent three storey tall Corinthian columns, remained operational as part of the Canadian Forces in the UK, and that closed in September 1947. A

(*f*) CMHQ had a little known alternative plan for Tweedsmuir Camp. On Monday, 26 June 1944, Major-General, The Honourable PJ Montague, Senior Officer at CMHQ, paid a surprise visit to the camp. In a memo to his Adjutant, Lieutenant-Colonel Louis Keene wrote:

Major-General PJ Montague, who inspected the camp late on Monday and early Tuesday, was pleased with the appearance of Tweedsmuir, which the General told me he had built for himself in case CMHQ was bombed out of London.

1 NETD / Lorne Scots War Diary / January to December 1944 - The National Archives

23

photograph of the detachment Colonel Keene commanded in Tweedsmuir Camp is shown in Fig. 2:2. Among their number was B51404 Bernard (Bern) Keegan, who was promoted through the ranks to sergeant. In the photograph he is standing second row from the top, fifth from the left. Sergeant Keegan served in Tweedsmuir Camp as a member of the Provost Military Police.

> We packed up and moved from Erie Camp to Tweedsmuir Camp in Thursley, Surrey about 20 miles away by transport. This was another new camp - excellent facilities with no complaints and much larger than Erie Camp. We settled into our new quarters, which had stoves, showers and hot water.

Sergeant Bernard Keegan

The photograph was taken in Guillemont Barracks, Cove, Hampshire in 1940. Prior to this, the unit was at Seaforth Barracks in Liverpool, transferring after a brief stay to Formby Camp near Freshfield in Lancashire, and about three weeks later from there by motor transport to Oulton Park, Cheshire. From Cheshire the unit was transferred yet again to Erie Camp on the Headley Downs before finally arriving by motor transport at Tweedsmuir Camp on 10 December 1941. During the five and

• **Fig. 2:2**

half years at Tweedsmuir Camp there were few changes to the personnel who were referred to by CMHQ as *Personnel on Permanent Employment* (or PE Staff).

Other than being invited by Admiral Hamilton to attend a Dinner Dance on 28 November 1942 at his Thursley home in aid of the 'Prisoners of War Fund', 1 NETD personnel kept very much to themselves that year. It was not until the start of 1943 that the Canadian Army unit at Tweedsmuir Camp started to mix with the village community. Some examples are a belated Christmas/New Year party for children in the NAAFI on 21 January, a number of garden fetes during the summer months, and High Tea arranged for civilians on 12 September at the Sergeant's Mess. Children's Christmas parties became a memorable event for many of the local children (ʃ). Recently Mr Ted Bates who, as a child, lived with his family in Homefield Cottages near St Michael and All Angels church, Thursley from 1945 to 1959, explained that he and his family have many happy memories of Christmas parties at Tweedsmuir Camp.

The officers of 1 NETD formed a strong working relationship with Sir Bruce Thomas who owned and lived in Dye House, which stands immediately opposite the camp's southern entrance. Two events are particularly worthy of being mentioned as examples of this friendship. On 26 June a "Prisoners of War fete was held at Dye House", which was "opened and attended by Field Marshal Lord Ironside." This is an especially important event to mention because Lord Edmund Ironside met John Buchan during WWI. In his book *The Thirty Nine Steps* Buchan's main character, Richard Hannay, is reputed to have been based on a young Edmund Ironside. Moreover, in 1940 Ironside was instrumental in devising the General Headquarters Anti-tank Line that became known as the GHQ Stop Line. The GHQ Stop Line ran through Elstead. When in 1941 Tweedsmuir Camp was being constructed by RCE, a plan was devised for sections of the RCE Battalions to man the Stop Line in the event of an enemy invasion.

> (ʃ) Children's Christmas parties at Tweedsmuir were organised by the camp's officers. Around £80 (sterling), a large amount of money in the 1940s, was usually allocated for the purchase of gifts and sweets. About fifty children attended each year. They were shown cartoon films ('Mickey Mouse', 'Popeye' and the like), and on one occasion a Punch and Judy show before settling down to a meal "of good things dear to the heart of children." Following the meal, "Santa Claus in the person of" either Captain Ferris or Major KM Johnson, both of whom were of the "appropriate shape and size", distributed the gifts. A bag of sweets was given to each child as they left for home with their parents.
>
> 1 NETD / Lorne Scots War Diaries - The National Archives

The second event occurred on 1 July when Sir Bruce helped to "cut the grass in front of the Officers' Mess to make it playable for golf practice." The lawn, as it was called in the early part of the 1940s (Fig. 2:3), exists to this day and is used occasionally by a local farmer for his herds of cattle.

There is nothing about the remains of the Officers' Mess to suggest that they once entertained some of the most important Canadian military and local dignitaries. A mass of nettles and a disconnected water pipe (Fig. 2:4) are as close as one can get to a building that was arguably one the most impressive structures on the site.

• Fig. 2:3

Together, the lawn and Officers' Mess were central to 1 NETD social diary. For example, on Sunday, 20 August 1944 a Garden Tea Dance was held in the Officers' Mess and marquees specially erected for the occasion. Over 100 guests were present who danced in the Mess to the music of an orchestra and afterwards were served tea in the marquees. Among those present were Major-General JH Roberts, Brigadiers Shields and MacDonald, Sir Bruce Thomas, Vice-Admiral and Mrs Hamilton, and Mr J Lomax, Chief Treasury Officer. The cheerful nature of the occasion was probably heard for miles around. Standing within the boundary of the site today, it is difficult to imagine such an occasion and the

• Fig. 2:4

26

friendship that obviously existed between the Canadian soldiers and the local community.

The August Garden Tea Dance had, of course, been arranged 75 days after the launch of Operation *Overlord*, or D-Day. From the 1 NEDT War Diaries, there seems to have been a sense of relief in Tweedsmuir Camp that the immediate dangers of war were finally dissolving at a rapid pace. As administrators of the camp, the Lorne Scots had witnessed four months of strict security, the arrival of Royal Air Force platoons "for small arms practice" at the indoor firing range (Fig.2:5), and the appearance of "a detachment of Churt Home Guard" under the command of David Lloyd-George's head gardener, all of whom "fired on the 30 yard range" (Fig. 2:6). They had also implemented numerous CMHQ directives that instructed officers commanding military camps in the UK to put into place detailed arrangements in support of the D-Day offensive. At last, in late August 1944, they could allow themselves to cast one eye towards Canada and think of the day when they would leave for home.

• Fig. 2:5

• Fig. 2:6

Interestingly, the upkeep of the camp during World War Two was the responsibility of two civilians: Mr William (Bill) Arrow and his handyman, Percy (no surname available) both of whom were local residents . They operated from a workshop near the motor transport garage adjacent to the Thursley Road entrance.

In Fig. 2:7, standing with his arm extended against his car is Bill Arrow, the camp's Clerk of Works. Behind him is Percy. Sitting on the bumper is Private Tommy Philips, Telephone Operator, and to the extreme right is Private Larry Stephens. Both Philips and Stephens served in the Lorne Scots at Tweedsmuir.

Using civilians as caretaker handymen gave the WO opportunities to ensure that there was continuity in running the camp's services efficiently. Although military personnel could easily have fulfilled the same duties, the uncertainty of whether a soldier would be in the camp from one day to the next presented obvious administrative issues.

• Fig. 2:7

A small number of Canadian servicemen in the camp married local English women, having met them at a dance or a local event in Thursley village. In Fig. 2:8, for example, are Private Larry Stephens and his wife holding their son, Barry. Next to Mrs Stephens is Private John Turner's wife, Irene. Both Mrs Stevens and Mrs Turner lived in Thursley cottages while their Canadian husbands were stationed in Tweedsmuir Camp.

According to Veterans Affairs of Canada, 48,000 young English women married Canadian servicemen between 1942 and 1947. Most of them and their 22,000 children went to live in Canada after the war.

The four photographs on the next page have been chosen to illustrate the appearance of Tweedsmuir Camp during the war.

• Fig. 2:8

28

- **Fig. 2:9** Left to Right:
  Private Ed South (an American),
  Private Laury Maury: Cook
  Private Larry Stephens

- **Fig. 2:10** Sergeant Bernard Keegan. In the background stands the timber built guardhouse, which in 1943 was replaced by a brick built guardhouse

- **Fig. 2:11** Left: Lt. Col. RW Lent
  Right: Col. RV Conover.
  (Conover was on a visit from Canada)

- **Fig. 2:12** Corporal Ewing and Mrs Graham (Motor Transport garage in background)

29

Chapter 3

Participation of Poland in WWII and the consequences of the Yalta Conference

• Remains of an indoor pistol range. To the back of this building was a brick backstop lined with sand bags

This chapter provides an overview of the Polish Forces contribution to World War Two and the consequences of the Yalta Conference, which was effectively to 'rubber stamp' the principles agreed at the Teheran Conference.

Poland's defence plan in 1939 was based on Poland holding out for at least two weeks, during which time Poland's allies, Britain and France, were expected to begin military operations along Germany's western border. If Germany was fighting on two fronts, it was anticipated that the German assault on Poland could be repulsed. Unfortunately, these operations were not feasible consequently no German divisions needed to be transferred from the Polish front. As soon as Moscow received news that Japan had agreed a truce over Manchuria, where Soviet Forces were in the field, Moscow ordered an attack on Poland's eastern border, a secretly agreed plan between Berlin and Moscow, known as the Molotov-Ribbentrop Pact.

Despite the catastrophic 'Polish Defence War' of 1939 (known as the September Campaign), when the Polish Forces collapsed within five weeks in the face of a German and a Soviet assault, the Polish Government (now in exile) decided to stay in the war. It went about re-grouping its forces outside Poland and deploying them alongside Allied troops, notably the French and the British. Subsequently, Polish Forces took part in the Battle of Britain (where one in eight RAF pilots was Polish), the Italian, French and North African campaigns, the Battle of the Atlantic, and the Normandy Landings (See pages 34-39). Also Polish cryptologists worked with the Special Operations Executive (SOE) stationed in Britain and occupied Europe. The intention after the war was for these forces to return to a liberated Polish Republic alongside the Polish Exiled Government.

Fig. 3:1 Photo call after the Yalta meetings of February 1945. Left to Right: Churchill, Roosevelt, Stalin

The reasons behind the existence of the Polish community in Tweedsmuir Camp are rooted in the Great Power politics of 1943-45.

4 February 1945 is not a date well known in the annals of the Second World War, whereas, in reality it was a defining moment in the development of post-war Eastern Europe. With Nazi Germany on the verge of defeat, the Allies (America, Britain and the Soviet Union), gathered to agree a peace settlement. This conference took place at Yalta in the Crimea, where the principal concern was to confirm the decisions made at Teheran in October 1943.

The Yalta conference addressed questions on the treatment of Germany after the war, the formation of the United Nations, the Polish question, the war in the Pacific and the opening of a Western Front. The issue of Poland, whose invasion by Germany led to Britain's declaration of war, received particular attention and saw the Soviet Union make demands on the country's self-determination and territory. For the Polish Government exiled in London the situation was clear: Moscow had no right to make any demands on the

Fig. 3:2 Flag of the United Nations (UN). The UN was officially established on 24 October 1945

31

Polish Republic.

Churchill, who had to be seen supporting the London Polish administration (as Poland had been an ally since 1939), trod a very thin line and bristled when it became clear that Stalin would not allow Polish diplomats to attend any meetings. Churchill was powerless to resist Soviet demands and so Poland was placed in the Soviet 'sphere of interest' and the 'Curzon Line' was adopted as Poland's new eastern border (see Fig. 3:3). This resulted in a part of pre-war Poland being annexed by the USSR and the installation of the Soviet sponsored Provisional Government of National Unity (PGNU), which had been established in the Polish capital to rival the exiled Polish Allied Government in London. Although Poland was compensated with German territory in the north and west, individuals who had originated from the east of Poland before the war would have found it difficult to return home.

Curzon Line

First mentioned by Lord Curzon in 1919, which identified Poland's proposed eastern border after The Great War

- **Fig. 3:3** .... Poland 1939
  ——————— Poland 1945

The Polish Government in exile protested loudly against the decisions adopted at Yalta regarding post-war Poland, and on 13 February 1945 officially refused to accept them. The grounds for refusal were, that it was not consulted, that no other nation had the right to pronounce on the future of the Polish allied government, that the sovereignty of Poland's territory was an internal (Polish) matter, and that the Polish Forces had not fought for their country only to be dictated to after the war. As far as the Polish allied authorities were concerned, these were irrefutable principles that they would defend to the last.

Churchill returned from Yalta a discontented man and, although he was party to the conference, he too was troubled by some of the agreements adopted. The British Prime Minister was deeply concerned by the spread of communism in Central Europe. Having gone to war to remove one totalitarian state (Nazi Germany) from dominating Europe, all that seemed to be happening was that it was being replaced by another (Soviet Russia). Furthermore, he grew despondent when the Americans started blaming him for setting the British and American line of occupation in Germany too far to the west. He was also concerned that it would soon be realised that he had yielded to the Soviets on Poland.

Once Attlee's government officially recognised the PGNU in July 1945, the future of the Polish allied authorities exiled in London were doomed. For the men of the Polish Forces, who had fought on the Western Front in the name of the exiled Polish Government, the decision was whether to return to Poland, which was now under Soviet influence, or to seek a life in exile.

Of those who refused repatriation, some accepted resettlement in Great Britain. They arrived by ship between September 1946 and and April 1948, where they joined Polish Forces already stationed there. Polish refugees, namely women, children and the elderly, who were displaced through the German and Soviet occupation of Poland and had spent much of the war in British safe-havens (such as India, Rhodesia and Tanganyika) or German concentration camps, were also allowed to settle in Britain, raising the number of Polish nationals in post-war Britain to approximately 200,000. Of these 114,037 Polish military personnel enlisted in the PRC, of whom a little over 91,000 (men and women) decided to remain in Britain.

• **Fig. 3:4** Provisional Government of National Unity Manifesto published in 1944

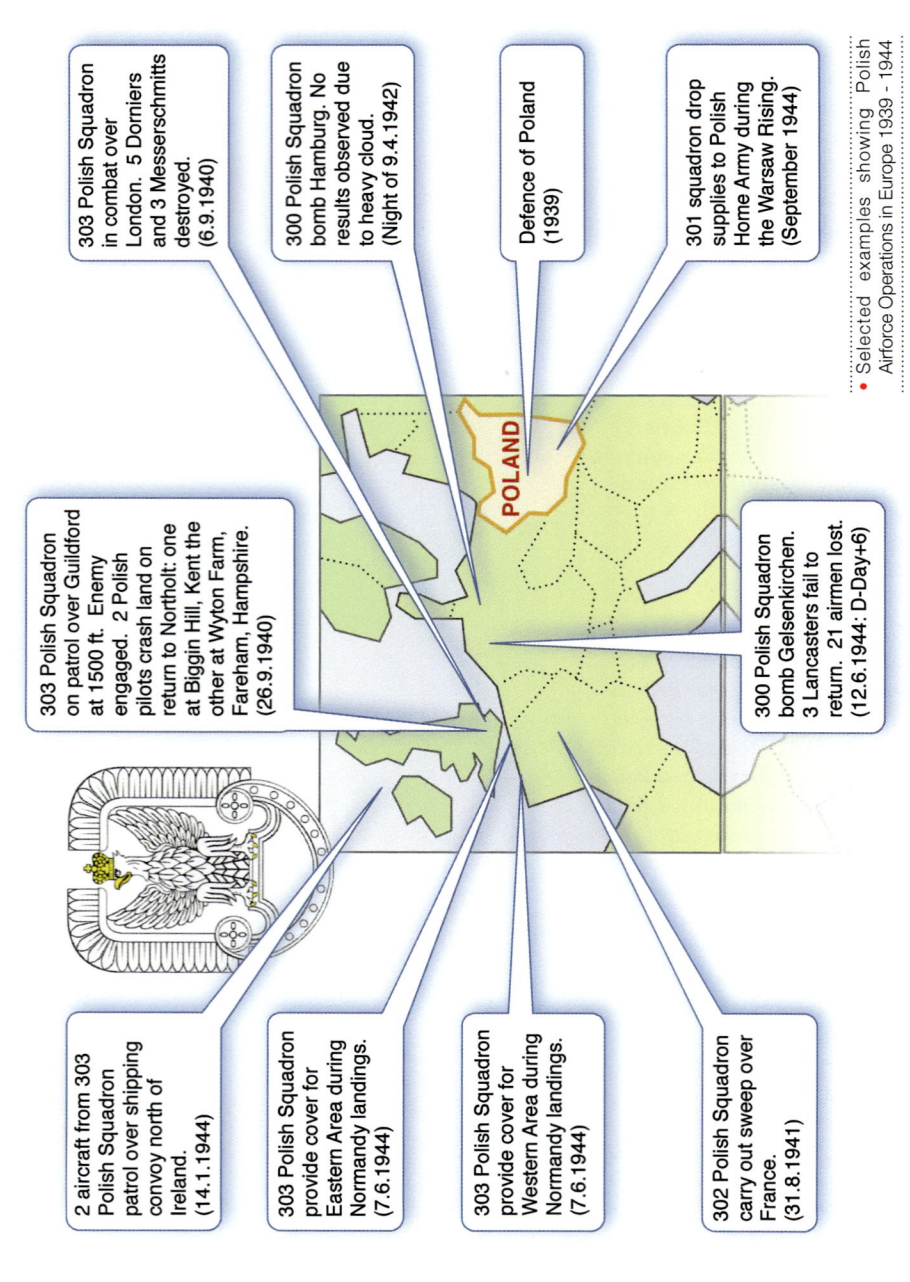

- 303 Polish Squadron in combat over London. 5 Dorniers and 3 Messerschmitts destroyed. (6.9.1940)

- 300 Polish Squadron bomb Hamburg. No results observed due to heavy cloud. (Night of 9.4.1942)

- Defence of Poland (1939)

- 301 squadron drop supplies to Polish Home Army during the Warsaw Rising. (September 1944)

- 303 Polish Squadron on patrol over Guildford at 1500 ft. Enemy engaged. 2 Polish pilots crash land on return to Northolt: one at Biggin Hill, Kent the other at Wyton Farm, Fareham, Hampshire. (26.9.1940)

- 300 Polish Squadron bomb Gelsenkirchen. 3 Lancasters fail to return. 21 airmen lost. (12.6.1944: D-Day+6)

- 2 aircraft from 303 Polish Squadron patrol over shipping convoy north of Ireland. (14.1.1944)

- 303 Polish Squadron provide cover for Eastern Area during Normandy landings. (7.6.1944)

- 303 Polish Squadron provide cover for Western Area during Normandy landings. (7.6.1944)

- 302 Polish Squadron carry out sweep over France. (31.8.1941)

• Selected examples showing Polish Airforce Operations in Europe 1939 - 1944

80% of Polish pilots survived after Poland fell to Nazi Germany and the Soviet Union in 1939. 9,276 of them crossed the border into Romania; 900 into Hungary; around 1,000 into Lithuania or Latvia, and some 1,500 were captured by the Soviets. In total nearly 10,000 Polish pilots made it to freedom: first in France, and then, when France fell, in Britain.

A large number of Polish pilots were detailed to report to Blackpool in Lancashire. There they experienced what official records report as 'Blackpoolitis' because the town was seen as a place that was as 'bad and demoralising' for them 'as some of Caesar's winter-quarters were for his legionaries'. Efforts were made to boost Polish pilots' morale by staging "let's be jolly activities'. (15.9.1940) (Today such activities would be referred to as *Team Building Events*.)

Polish airmen of all ranks were encouraged to observe Polish tradition by, for example, attending "Easter Church Service … followed by the traditional Polish Dinner" [sic].

Operation Ramrod to ensure the success of the Normandy invasion. (August 1944)

Romania was Poland's ally but, during the war, Nazi Germany made efforts to break that alliance. Polish pilots began a long trek through Romanian concentration camps, clearing depots and the like, which continued for over a year. The pilots 'became demoralised' particularly by the time they arrived in Britain to be quartered in yet more camps.

The team building events included activities such as Tic-Tac-Toe, sports and singing in a choir.

On 3 March 1944 the first crew of the 300 Polish Squadron completed its "conversion training' from Wellington to Lancaster aircraft at No.1 Lancaster Finishing School, RAF, Hemswell, Lincolnshire".

Polish pilots report 'red, white and blue parachutes all over Utah Beach and 10 miles inland' as American Airborne Units are deployed on the Cotentin peninsula in support of, and before, the American landings at Normandy.

Polish pilots report extensive fires on Omaha and Gold Beaches. 'Intensive opposition' on Omaha in evidence. (6.6.1944)

4 spitfires of 303 squadron led by Flt. Sgt. J Stasik provide cover for Transport No. 48 to Airport A.9 in Normandy with Allied **Supreme Commander Dwight Eisenhower** as passenger. (D-day + 66)

D-day + 66: The RAF was now flying fewer operational sorties and an increased number of training sorties before being stood down from war duties.

- Other examples of Polish Airforce Operations and Events

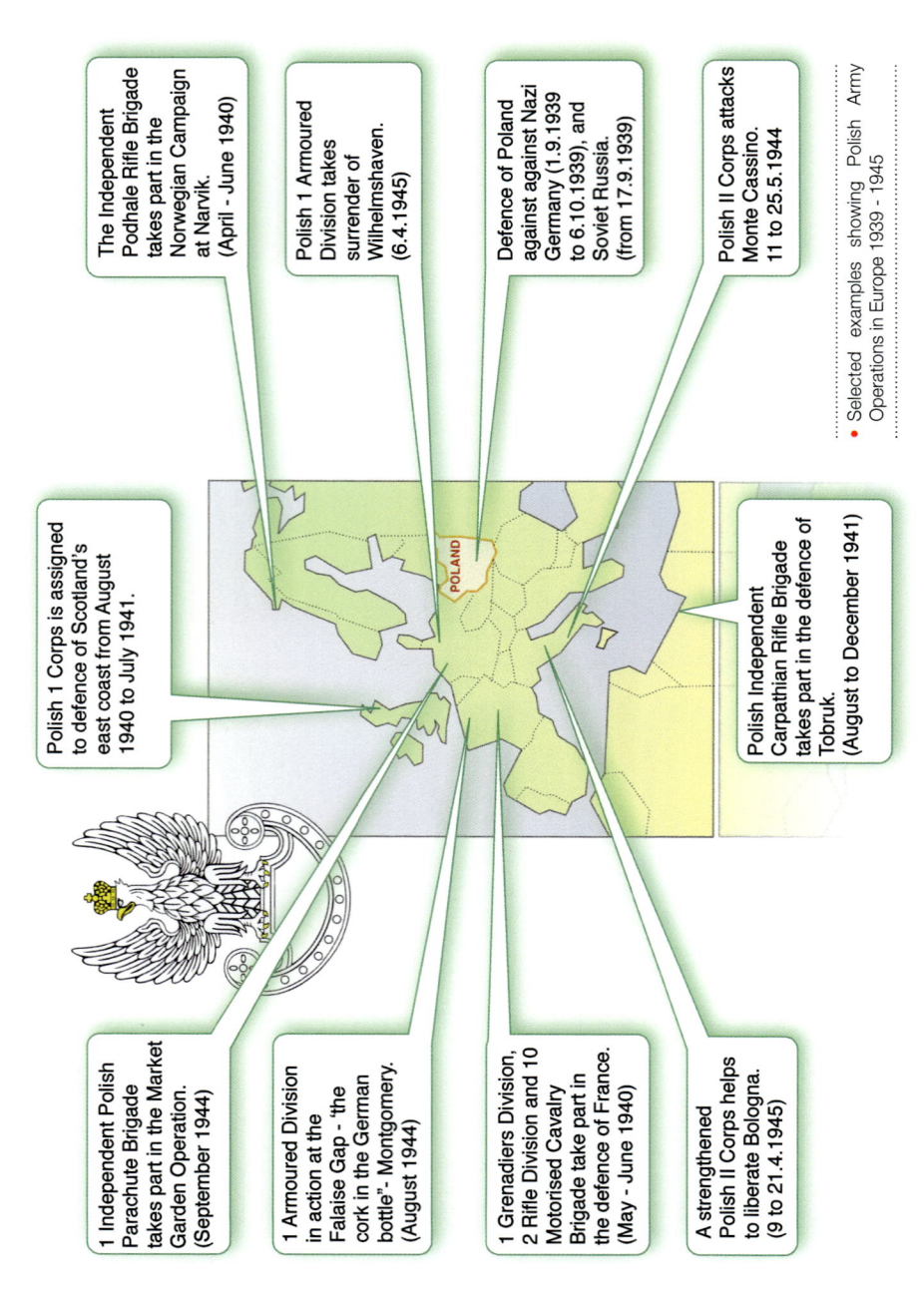

- The Independent Podhale Rifle Brigade takes part in the Norwegian Campaign at Narvik. (April - June 1940)

- Polish 1 Armoured Division takes surrender of Wilhelmshaven. (6.4.1945)

- Defence of Poland against against Nazi Germany (1.9.1939 to 6.10.1939), and Soviet Russia. (from 17.9.1939)

- Polish II Corps attacks Monte Cassino. 11 to 25.5.1944

- Selected examples showing Polish Army Operations in Europe 1939 - 1945

- Polish 1 Corps is assigned to defence of Scotland's east coast from August 1940 to July 1941.

- Polish Independent Carpathian Rifle Brigade takes part in the defence of Tobruk. (August to December 1941)

- 1 Independent Polish Parachute Brigade takes part in the Market Garden Operation. (September 1944)

- 1 Armoured Division in action at the Falaise Gap - "the cork in the German bottle" - Montgomery. (August 1944)

- 1 Grenadiers Division, 2 Rifle Division and 10 Motorised Cavalry Brigade take part in the defence of France. (May - June 1940)

- A strengthened Polish II Corps helps to liberate Bologna. (9 to 21.4.1945)

36

- The last military battle in the defence of Poland occurred on 4 October 1939 when the last unit surrendered.

- Around 90,000 Polish troops fled Poland after the country fell in October 1939. Of these some 30,000 were in Romania, 40,000 in Hungary, 14,000 in Lithuania and 1,500 in Latvia.

- Thousands of Polish citizens, including Prisoners of War, were transported either west to German work camps, or east to Soviet concentration camps.

- Members of the Polish Government were interned in Hungary.

- A prior agreement between France and Poland allowed Polish troops to evacuate to France or French territories such as Syria.

- A new Polish government was restructured in France under the prime ministership of General Wadysaw Sikorski. He was also the supreme head of Poland's Forces. A training camp at Coëtquidan in Brittany became the base for a new Polish Army.

- A Franco-Polish Military Agreement was signed on 4 January 1940, bringing the Polish Forces under French Operational Command.

- When France fell the Polish Forces evacuated to Britain from where the Polish Navy was already operating. The Polish Army was quartered in barracks in Scotland. These troops formed the 1st Polish Armoured Division, which in 1945 was reformed as the I Polish Corps.

- On 5 August 1940 an Anglo-Polish Military Agreement was signed. The agreement was ratified on 22 August by the Allied Forces Act.

- In June 1941 Nazi Germany attacked Soviet Russia. Fearing annihilation, Soviet Russia sided with the Western Allies. Poland signed a new agreement with the USSR, permitting the release of Polish citizens and Prisoners of War from Soviet concentration camps.

- In early 1942 the Prisoners of War, and other Polish citizens released from Soviet camps, join the newly formed Polish Army on Soviet Russian soil. Some formations evacuate to the Middle East for training.

- Polish formations fought alongside Australian, British, and Canadian troops.

- After the war, many thousands of Polish people returned to Poland. The troops of the Polish II Corps, now in Italy, refused, arguing that their country had been decimated and their homes confiscated by the USSR. They were transferred to Britain. Some of them ended up temporarily in Tweedsmuir Camp before making a life for their families elsewhere.

- **Fig. 3:6** Other examples of Polish Army Operations and Events

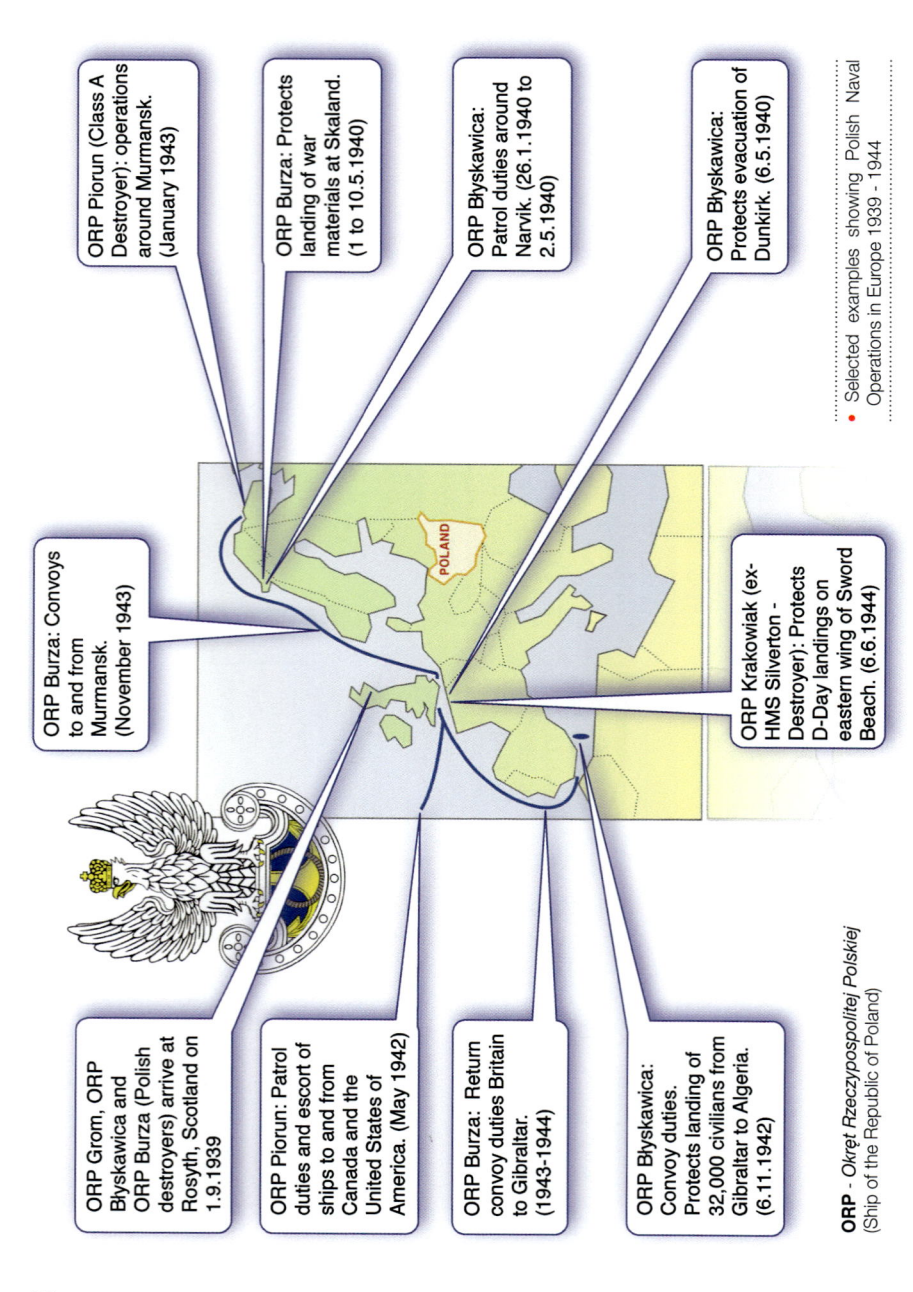

- ORP Piorun (Class A Destroyer): operations around Murmansk. (January 1943)
- ORP Burza: Protects landing of war materials at Skaland. (1 to 10.5.1940)
- ORP Błyskawica: Patrol duties around Narvik. (26.1.1940 to 2.5.1940)
- ORP Błyskawica: Protects evacuation of Dunkirk. (6.5.1940)
- ORP Burza: Convoys to and from Murmansk. (November 1943)
- ORP Krakowiak (ex-HMS Silverton - Destroyer): Protects D-Day landings on eastern wing of Sword Beach. (6.6.1944)
- ORP Grom, ORP Błyskawica and ORP Burza (Polish destroyers) arrive at Rosyth, Scotland on 1.9.1939
- ORP Piorun: Patrol duties and escort of ships to and from Canada and the United States of America. (May 1942)
- ORP Burza: Return convoy duties Britain to Gibraltar. (1943-1944)
- ORP Błyskawica: Convoy duties. Protects landing of 32,000 civilians from Gibraltar to Algeria. (6.11.1942)

- Selected examples showing Polish Naval Operations in Europe 1939 - 1944

ORP - *Okręt Rzeczypospolitej Polskiej* (Ship of the Republic of Poland)

38

Other examples of Polish Naval Operations and Events

- ORP Grom, ORP Burza and ORP Błyskawica at Rosyth, Scotland. ORP Iskra at Casablanca, ORP Wilk and ORP Orzeł (both submarines) in British waters. (At start of the war)

- Commanding Officer, Destroyer Division, Roman Stankiewicz invited to meet 1st Lord of the Admiralty, Winston Churchill and 1st Sea Lord, Dudley Pound. (4.9.1940)

- ORP Błyskawica entered the service of the 5 British Destroyer Flotilla under the command of Captain Lord Louis Mountbatten. (6.9.1940)

- ORP Garland (RN G-Class Destroyer, transferred to the Polish Navy in May 1940): Damaged on 27.5.1942 in air attack during Murmansk run. Several Polish sailors were killed or injured. One dying sailor had written in his own blood "*Polsko, dla Ciebie słodko ...*" (English: How sweet it is to die for you Poland …).

- Doctor from ORP Burza is winched to Aconit (French Frigate) in mid Atlantic to provide medical assistance to injured from HMS Harvester (RN Destroyer), which had sunk the previous day. (12.3.1943)

- American, British and French vessels were transferred to the Polish Navy. For example, the submarine ORP Jastrząb (ex-USS S-25), ORP Piorun (ex-HMS Nerissa), ORP Garland (ex-HMS Garland), and ORP Ouragan (ex-French).

- ORP Piorun took part in operation to hunt down the battleship Bismarck. Reports show that Piorun was the first to locate the whereabouts of the German battleship during the night of 25-26 May 1941.

- ORP Ślązak (ex-HMS Bedale - Hunt II Class Destroyer): Took part in 'Operation Jubilee', the ill-fated Dieppe Assault. Its losses counted 3 dead and 12 wounded. Played key role in returning to Portsmouth injured Canadian soldiers (18 to 20.8.1942)

  On 18 August Ślązak took a direct hit. 3 Polish sailors were killed and 12 injured.

- The Polish Merchant Navy played its role in the evacuation of Dunkirk beaches, transporting American and Canadian Forces across the Atlantic and participating in various landing operations.

- Polish Navy ceased to operate in May 1945.

Chapter 4

Transfer from the Polish Armed Forces to the Polish Resettlement Corps: an unarmed British unit

- Remains of excavated ground upon which once stood a timber framed barracks (June 2005)

When the Second World War ended, the men and women of the Polish Forces faced a dilemma: to return to Poland, go to Britain or migrate to a third country. This eight page chapter outlines the events that led to their dilemma.

When the war in Europe ended in May 1945, there was an estimated 250,000 Polish servicemen and women stationed in Austria, Britain, Germany and the Middle East under British operational command. The expectation was that all Polish units would return to their country. According to Keith Sword, 54% of "the troops returned to Poland ... or migrated to third countries." The vast majority of those who returned, especially those in the Polish Army, had roots in Polish provinces that lay west of the Curzon Line. The remainder, those whose familial origins were predominantly from regions east of the Curzon Line, usually referred to as *Kresy* (Fig. 4:1), opted for transfer to Britain where they continued to be encouraged to repatriate. Those who remained in Britain were formed into a non-combatant unit called the Polish Resettlement Corps (PRC) for the sole purpose of giving them the chance to find work and make a smooth transition into civilian life, whether in Britain or a country other than Poland.

- Fig. 4:1

40

The fact that the PRC was formed in Great Britain is arguably due to two main events. The first was a response by Winston Churchill on 27 February 1945 to the unease over political developments in eastern Europe. The British premier effectively offered the chance of settlement in Britain and the British Empire to individuals of Polish formations under British command who felt unable to return to their homeland. According to Keith Sword, this *pledge*, as it became known in Whitehall, "overshadowed all subsequent … efforts to limit the settlement of Poles in Britain."

Churchill's *pledge* caused confusion for Whitehall staff as it referred only to men in the Polish Forces who had seen action under British operational command. All other Polish servicemen who had fought only in Poland in the 1939 Campaign or who had been recruited in, but not left, Britain were considered ineligible to be included in the Corps. Neither could women in the auxiliary services nor civilians. In the end, however, an amicable compromise had to be found. In a publication called *Polish Resettlement Corps: Procedure for Relegation*, the WO made this statement.

> Reckonable service will include only that service rendered with the Polish Forces under British Command, ie within the period 1 July 1940 to 15 August 1946. NO service is reckonable in the case of Poles who entered the Polish Forces after 31 May 1945.

This was followed by the creation of a separate unit for Polish women who had served in any one of the three services during the war. They were demobilised through the Polish Auxiliary Territorial Service/Polish Resettlement Section (ATS/PRS). 'Section' and not 'Corps' was the preferred common noun for the Auxiliary Services (see also page 52).

• Fig. 4:2

The second event was the British General Election of July 1945 in which Clement Attlee was unexpectedly elected as Prime Minister, leading a Labour Party that promised, among other social reforms, new housing, a 'cradle-to-grave' welfare system, and a national health service. These required bold steps, which wiped the domestic political slate clean and accepted the new European order as outlined at Yalta in readiness for the inauguration of new horizons for Britain. The outcome of the General Election, it could be argued, removed the largely stable and trusting relationship that had developed between Churchill's coalition government and the Polish military and civilian hierarchy during the war.

Although the 1945 General Election results were known at Whitehall prior to their declaration on 25 July, the official pronouncement had to wait until after the votes from personnel in the British Forces abroad had been returned and counted. For the interim period a "Caretaker" Government, as James Chuter-Ede (Britain's Home Secretary) called it in 1947, was installed. Winston Churchill remained Prime Minister until the King was advised by Clement Attlee that, as leader of the Labour Party, he could form the next government. At that point Attlee was the 'prime-minister-in-waiting'. His Foreign Secretary was to be Ernest Bevin. One of Bevin's immediate objectives during the interim period was to make it clear to his Foreign Office (FO) officials that he was anxious for Britain to establish working relations with the PGNU and that the undertakings of the Potsdam Conference, which started on 17 July and finished on 2 August 1945, were carried out. This was the final conference of the leaders of Great Britain, the United States and the Union of Soviet Socialist Republics before the Council of Foreign Ministers conducted conferences on the peace settlement between September 1945 in London, and June 1949 in Paris. Potsdam was the conference at which Clement Attlee took over as British Prime Minister from Winston Churchill as by then the 1945 General Election results had been announced.

It was within this context that, during the "Caretaker" government's tenure, the FO made three recommendations following Bevin's instruction, all of which were discharged before the 1945 election results were made public. The first was to establish an *Interim Treasury Committee* (ITC) for Polish Affairs. Its responsibility was to oversee the removal of the London based Polish Government from the national and international political scenes, and to attend to the needs of Polish orphans, disabled people and other refugees scattered around the world thus reducing the risk of a humanitarian disaster. The ITC was a civilian body, comprising both British civil servants and employees of the Polish Government familiar with the administrative procedures of its departments. The second was to acknowledge the PGNU as the legal government of Poland. The third recommendation was to form a *Polish Armed Forces Committee* (PAFC). Its brief was similar to that of the ITC, but with respect to Poland's Forces who had fought under British operational command. While so doing, the PAFC was also attempting to persuade all personnel of the Polish Armed Forces to repatriate.

All three recommendations were completed within 14 days of each other: on 5 July an announcement was made that diplomatic recognition had been transferred from the Polish Government in London to the PGNU in Warsaw; on 6 July the ITC first met, and on 19 July the PAFC first met.

These three initiatives were to have paved the way for transferring the administration of the ITC and the PAFC as "organs" of Polish civilians' welfare, and Polish Forces' welfare to the Warsaw authorities.

The process of repatriation, however, did not run smoothly. It was hindered by the refusal of the Polish Forces to accept not just the terms agreed at the three allied conferences of Teheran, Yalta and Potsdam, but also the de-recognition of the government, in whose name they had fought, for just over five years. Anxious for the repatriation programme to succeed, Britain persuaded the PGNU that together they should formulate an encouraging statement for the Polish Forces (stationed in Austria, Britain, France, Germany, Italy, the Middle East and Switzerland), advising them that they had nothing to fear upon their return to Poland. An agreed statement was signed on 4 February 1946. However, on 14 February the PGNU announced that it "no longer considered the land, sea and air formations in the west to be units of the Polish Forces." Any airman, sailor or soldier, wishing to return to Poland would have to do so as an individual at Polish Consulates abroad; in effect, the Polish servicemen were to be treated as civilians and their citizenship called into question. At the same time, the Soviet FO had forwarded to the General Secretary of the United Nations a memorandum, alleging that "the presence of Polish troops on the Italian- Yugoslav border constituted a threat to peace in the region." For the British this was becoming a diplomatic embarrassment, which had to be resolved. One of the first objectives was to establish how much it was costing to keep the Polish units.

When Lord Keynes, a leading economist of the day, demonstrated to Attlee in February 1946 that running the Polish Army alone was costing Britain £2.5 million per month, the Prime Minister immediately set up a *Cabinet Polish Forces Committee* (CPFC), which took over responsibilities from the PAFC. The primary objective of the CPFC was "the disposal of (the) Polish forces." Chairing the committee, which met for the first time on 4 April, was Hugh Dalton, Chancellor of the Exchequer. The fact that the Chair was a finance minister strongly implies that Attlee's priority was to disband the Polish Armed Forces as cost effectively as possible. On 2 March Attlee made a statement to all his departments.

> We cannot tolerate any longer the grave political embarrassment, or the financial commitment involved by our maintenance of these forces under arms. The problem must be tackled and all Ministers concerned must be ready to make a contribution to its solution.

This was to become the basis upon which the PRC was formed and the *Polish Resettlement Act* of 1947 conceived.

On 15 March 1946 Attlee and Bevin met senior Polish commanders many of whom, including Commander-in-Chief, General Władysław Anders, whose Polish II Corps was stationed at Ancona, Italy, wanted to retain the Polish Forces in tact. The Polish military leadership believed that this would give them the advantage of both bringing pressure to bear on Warsaw, and being ready for any conflict between West and East, which they believed was imminent. As the British side was aware of the Polish position, Attlee and Bevin wanted to make it clear that a decision had been made to disband the Polish Forces, and that a written statement to this effect would be circulated to the men. The Polish commanders protested. With the agreement of his Chiefs of Staff, Bevin then suggested that Anders be detained in Britain and not permitted to return to his troops unless he agreed to support British plans for the demobilisation of the Polish Forces. Anders agreed to comply. Senior Polish commanders' protestations may have been the result of having knowledge of Operation *Unthinkable*, an offensive that would have included a combined American, British, German and Polish force against the USSR, regarding it as the only way to bring back independence to Poland. Due to the nature of *Unthinkable*, the Chiefs of Staff agreed to commit as little as possible to paper. It is an issue that will be discussed more fully in Chapter 14 - Final Comments.

Five days later, on 20 March, Ernest Bevin relayed the situation as it was at the time to the House of Commons. He made it clear that he had discussed with the PGNU their declaration that they no longer regarded the units of the Polish Armed Forces under British command, as forming part of the Armed Forces of Poland, and advised the House that he had received "assurances from them (the PGNU) that it does not affect the conditions set out in the document which is being issued to the troops; that these conditions will still apply to all Polish troops returning from abroad; and that they will, as far as possible, deal with applicants for repatriation by categories rather than insist upon individual scrutiny by their consulates." He added that he would be issuing an accompanying note translated into Polish, stating that "His Majesty's Government regard the information set forth in the agreed document as satisfactory, and that they consider it to be the duty of all members of the (Polish) Forces to decide now to return to their own country." To Attlee and Bevin's disappointment, however, the documents had the opposite effect as members of the Polish Forces rebuffed them. There was disbelief and even anger that a British Cabinet Minister had the effrontery to advise them to return to Poland.

On 21 May the Foreign Secretary once again called a meeting with Polish senior officers, advising them of a plan that included Polish troops abroad being transported to Britain and the creation of a *Polish Resettlement Corps* (at this stage it was called the *Industrial Settlement Corps*). After his meeting with Anders, Bevin made a statement to the House of Commons on the following day, Wednesday, 22 May 1946, outlining the governments decision.

The graphic on the next page illustrates the major issues described in this chapter.

1945

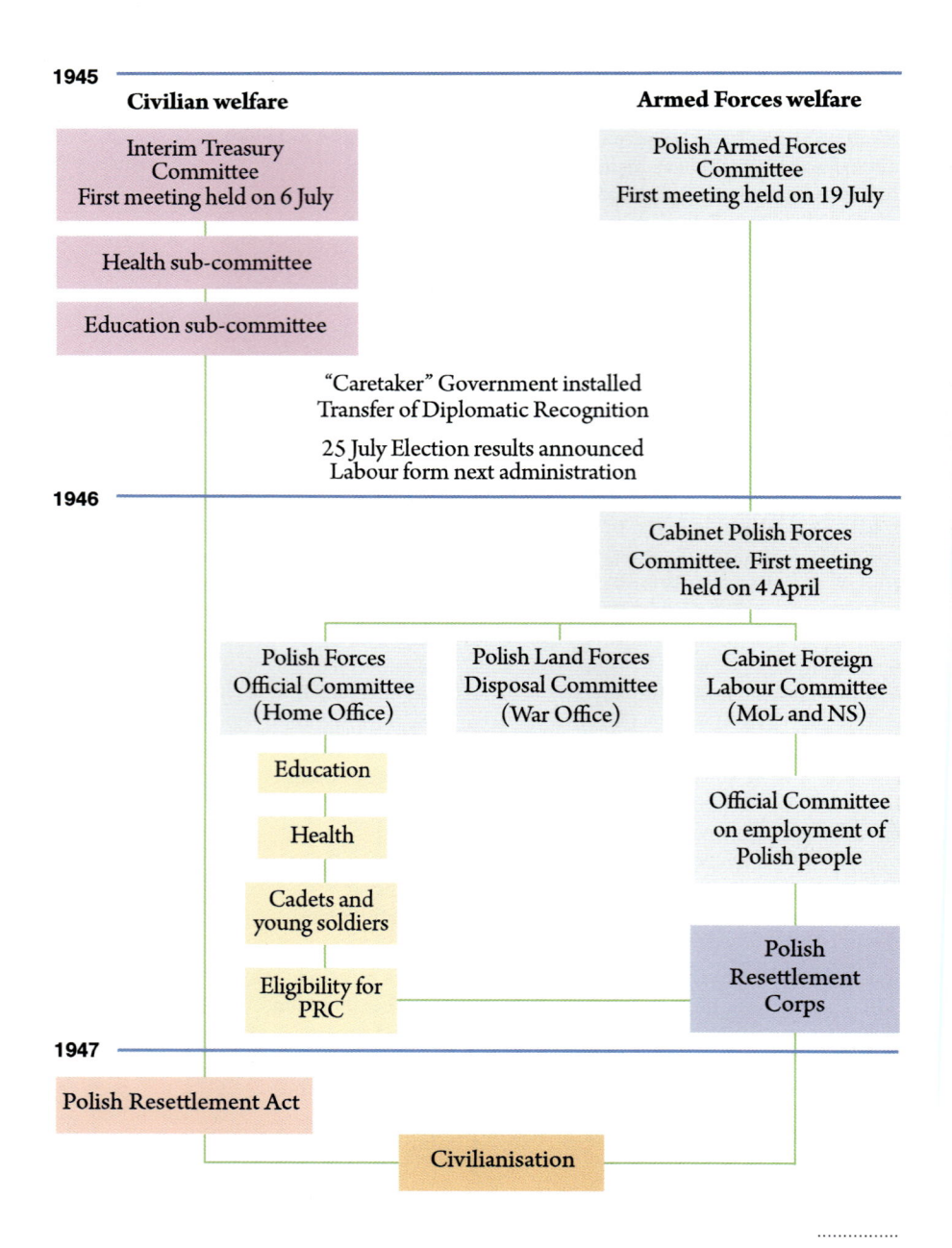

Civilian welfare	Armed Forces welfare
Interim Treasury Committee — First meeting held on 6 July	Polish Armed Forces Committee — First meeting held on 19 July

- Health sub-committee
- Education sub-committee

"Caretaker" Government installed
Transfer of Diplomatic Recognition

25 July Election results announced
Labour form next administration

1946

Cabinet Polish Forces Committee. First meeting held on 4 April

- Polish Forces Official Committee (Home Office)
- Polish Land Forces Disposal Committee (War Office)
- Cabinet Foreign Labour Committee (MoL and NS)

- Education
- Health
- Cadets and young soldiers
- Eligibility for PRC

Official Committee on employment of Polish people

Polish Resettlement Corps

1947

Polish Resettlement Act

Civilianisation

• Fig. 4:3

The troops of the Polish II Corps were among the first to have been transferred to Britain. It was a particularly well oiled procedure. Three months before their arrival on British shores, Holy Masses were said at places where the II Corps had been stationed. Their commander, General Władysław Anders, inspected units before saluting their contribution to the war effort (Figs. 4:4 to 4:7).

- **Figs. 4:4** Holy Mass at Casarano, Southern Italy on 16 June 1946 before transfer to Great Britain

- **Fig. 4:5** Final inspection of a Polish Army unit at Casarano, Southern Italy.

- **Fig.4:6** Boarding a ship, IItaly

- **Fig. 4:7** Marching in Prescot, Liverpool

47

Chapter 5

Families, Dependants and Orphans

• Remains of a lecture theatre that existed during the war, and converted to a nursery school after the war

Chapter 5 explains how Polish Resettlement Corps families were defined for ease of administration, their origins, and how they were distinguished from Polish Resettlement Corps dependants.

Six days before Churchill made his *pledge* to the House of Commons on 27 February 1945, he had had an "emotionally charged meeting with General Anders," wrote Keith Sword in 1989. "Churchill was clearly influenced by his encounter with Anders," continued Sword, when he made, what Sword considered to be the sudden pronouncement. Churchill spoke eloquently of "the Polish troops ... who had fought under British command." He had hoped "that it may be possible to offer (them) the citizenship and freedom of the British Empire ..." His emotions were fully charged when he spoke the last few words on the matter, saying that " ... we should think it an honour to have such faithful and valiant warriors dwelling among us as if they were our own flesh and blood." It was a statement that had barely been discussed by the War Cabinet, and certainly not with leaders of the Dominion countries. Yet Australia and Canada, for example, were urged to accept many thousands of men from the Polish Armed Force after the war.

The *pledge* made no mention of whether, the soldiers' families and relatives should be included. There were 396,147 Polish refugees accommodated in camps found in 30 countries that stretched from Sweden to Australia and Mexico to India. The problem facing the new Labour administration between 1946 and 1948 was which of the civilians should form part of the PRC process and on what grounds were they to be included. To begin with, the title "refugee", and subsequently "displaced person" continued to be used in correspondence and memoranda between British government departments until it became clear that a more precise definition was required to identify just who exactly Whitehall officials were dealing with. Hence a distinction was made between persons who could be regarded as PRC "family" members, and PRC "dependants."

A family member was the wife, child or children of a PRC enlistee. Other relatives such as uncles, aunts, cousins, mothers and fathers were described as dependants. Therefore, while men in the PRC lived in "Families Camps" with their wives and children, other relatives lived in "Dependants Camps."

There is no evidence to suggest that the ATS/PRS included married women with children. Had there been, then by definition they, their husbands and their children, would have been accommodated in Dependants Camps and not Families Camps.

• Fig. 5:1

It may be of interest to know that as well as "families" and "dependants", the Home Office also differentiated between other groups of Polish individuals for whom camps were prepared. For instance, Service Camps/PRC were prepared for single men; Service Camps/ATS(PRS) for single women; Recalcitrant Camps for Polish Airforce, Army and Navy personnel (men) who persistently refused to enlist into the PRC, and Disabled Camps for personnel (men) who had been wounded during the war and whose welfare depended on others.

We have found no evidence of Polish orphans at Tweedsmuir

even though the war had left many in the care of the Red Cross in countries often referred to as "safe havens" such as Uganda, India, Denmark and Sweden. In the main, the orphans were evacuated to Canada and New Zealand from the country that hosted their stay during the war. Some of them, however, remained in the care of their host country after the war.

During the immediate post war period, Tweedsmuir Camp became a Service Camp for PRC personnel, but was later reclassified as a Families Camp. As such only men (PRC or those demobilised from the PRC) with wives and children were to be accommodated there. However, owing to an administrative oversight, a few grandparents, and in some cases more distant relatives also settled in Tweedsmuir. It is therefore impossible to describe a typical family at Tweedsmuir Camp. Arguably, the best way to deal with this issue is to provide graphic summaries of the origins of families who settled at the camp.

All the 'Polish husbands' in the graphics below should be seen as examples of PRC enlistees who were demobilised at the end of September 1949.

```
POLISH HUSBAND     POLISH WIFE
         |              |
         Marry in Poland
                |
       Start a Family in Poland
                |
   Husband serves in Polish Army;
   arrive separately in Britain after
   WWII; are reunited and settle at
         Tweedsmuir Camp
```

```
POLISH HUSBAND     POLISH WIFE
         |              |
   Meet and marry in Britain after WWII
                |
            Start a Family
                |
       Settle at Tweedsmuir Camp
```

POLISH HUSBAND	POLISH WIFE

Meet in north Germany after WWII; marry in Italy; arrive separately to Britain and are reunited

Start a Family

Settle at Tweedsmuir Camp

POLISH WIFE

Marries in Poland; evacuated with children to safe haven; bereaved by war

Arrives in Britain after WWII; meets and marries

POLISH HUSBAND

Settles at Tweedsmuir Camp

Extends the Family

POLISH HUSBAND	POLISH WIFE

Marry in the Middle East; first born in the Middle East; evacuate to Britain at the end of WWII

Settle in Tweedsmuir Camp

Extend the Family

POLISH WIFE

Marries in Poland; evacuated with children to safe haven; bereaved by war

Arrives in Britain with children after WWII and is reunited

GRANDPARENT(S) OR MORE DISTANT RELATIVE(S)

Settle at Tweedsmuir Camp

Chapter 6

The Origins of Tweedsmuir Camp as a place for Resettlement

- 19th Century bridge built of brick and local stone. The bridge spanned a water management canal

This chapter illustrates Tweedsmuir Camp's unique history as a place of temporary resettlement for Polish ex-army personnel, which spawned a battle of words between the WO and the National Assistance Board (NAB).

As a Polish resettlement camp Tweedsmuir's history is unique because in 1947 it was the only WO camp in the United Kingdom that accommodated Polish ex-army personnel who were employed by the WO as administrators at Witley Camp responsible for demobilising personnel from the Polish Armed Forces. This process was mandated by the *Polish Resettlement Act* of 1947. While the WO was responsible for all PRC personnel, the *Polish Resettlement Act* removed from the ITC all activities associated with Polish families and dependants, and gave NAB officials overall responsibility for the welfare of all post-war Polish civilians in the UK. (The process of civilianising the PRC at Tweedsmuir Camp did not include Polish Air Force units or Polish Naval units because they were not accommodated there after the war.)

The formation of the PRC gave rise to completely new British units. Each Polish Army unit was renamed Brigade Group or Basic Unit. These names were preceded by a number. For example, 53 Brigade Group and 514 Basic Unit. There was also an assortment of miscellaneous army units such as 5 PRC Provost Company; 6 Medical Company; 472 Army Kit Stores (PRC), and 12 Court Martial (PRC). At the same time, each Polish ATS unit was organised as a Company, again preceded by a number. For instance, 53 Company (ATS/PRS). Sometimes, Whitehall replaced PRS with the PRC acronym.

As the Canadian Army was being repatriated in 1947, the War Office in London was making plans to transport all Polish servicemen and women, who opted to enlist in the PRC, to Britain for demobilisation. Hence at about the time when the *Polish Resettlement Act* was being read for the second time in the House of Commons, the WO made an announcement which included three crucial decisions that would impact on future events surrounding Tweedsmuir Camp until the late 1950s.

The first decision was to make Witley Camp (Fig. 6:1), a long established military institution, the Pay and Record Office, PRC. It would be there that records of enlisted Polish Servicemen and women were kept, and from where their service pay was distributed. The second decision was to keep Tweedsmuir Camp open to accommodate Polish ex-army personnel employed by the WO as PRC administrators. The third announcement stated that Polish Army personnel in Tweedsmuir would be civilianised by the War Office as and when the PRC started to shrink in size. When the NAB heard of these decisions it saw an opportunity to protect its purse and distance itself from Tweedsmuir, leaving the camp's management to the WO in London.

• **Fig. 6:1** Witley Camp to the left of the narrow London to Portsmouth Road (A3) - circa 1916

War Office procedures for administrating the PRC camps included a command structure that started at PRC Headquarters, Egerton Gardens, London, and ended with the Commanding Officers at PRC camps. Additionally England, Scotland, Wales, the Isle of Man and the Isle of Wight were divided into areas known as Home Commands. The officers commanding each command area were responsible for carrying out orders issued by PRC Headquarters. Occasionally clerical errors were made. For example, part of the boundary between Southern Command and Eastern Command was the border between Surrey and Hampshire. In June 1947 a typographical error placed Tweedsmuir near Hursley, Hampshire not Thursley, Surrey. Subsequently, in some documents, Tweedsmuir Camp was often sited in Southern Command and not, as it should have been, in Eastern Command (see Fig. 6:2).

Before transferring Polish servicemen and women to Britain, the WO put into place logistics systems that would ease the management of the 114,037 individuals who had decided to enlist in the PRC. The systems included individuals such as dentists, doctors, quartermasters and chefs. They also included 'hardware' such as, typewriters with Polish alphabet strikers, rubber stamps for administrative purposes (see Fig. 6:3), and surgical instruments. It would seem that the logistics systems had been assembled in Britain between June 1946 and September 1946, and that PRC staff had been assigned to where they were required before the larger numbers of Polish Army personnel were transferred to Britain. For instance, some of the surgeons and their equipment were sent to No. 6 Polish Hospital, Diddington Camp in Eastern England, and typewriters to Witley Camp, Surrey.

While enrolment into the PRC began with the Polish II Corps from Italy on 13 September 1946, the final group of Polish soldiers were transferred from the Middle East to Britain in April 1948. But the first Polish soldiers to

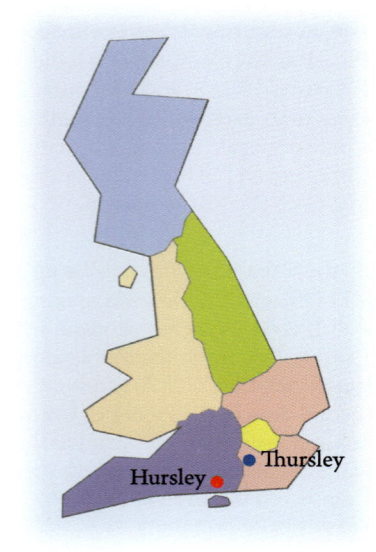

Scottish Command
Western Command
Southern Command
Eastern Command
London Command (HQ)
Northern Command

• Fig. 6:2

• Fig. 6:3

arrive at Tweedsmuir were the men of the 55 Brigade Group, PRC who entered the camp on 7 July 1947, five months after the evacuation of the last Canadian soldier. Four days later, on 11 July, personnel of the 501 Basic Unit were accommodated at the camp under the command of Lieutenant-Colonel Berendt.

The 55 Brigade Group comprised volunteers from the Polish Land Forces for the newly created *Placement in Employment in the Merchant Navy* scheme, and were in transit to either Portsmouth or Southampton. The 501 were staff employed by the WO at the PRC Pay and Record Office, Witley Camp. While the 55 Brigade Group left Tweedsmuir on 12 December 1947, some individuals of the 501 unit occupied barracks at the camp into the 1950s.

Among their number was Sergeant Stanisław Lis (Fig. 6:4) who was employed as Quartermaster, Witley Camp, PRC. He and his young family left Tweedsmuir in 1951 to settle in London. By this time the PRC had been run down and Sergeant Lis was keen to find work. He had qualified as a saddle maker in Poland before the war, and was seeking to secure a position in the leather industry, reasoning that London would provide better opportunities.

Fig. 6:4 Sergeant Lis with his wife Janina and their son Zbigniew (Bish)

Not all Polish staff at Witley lived in Tweedsmuir Camp. Some, like Franciszek Szuta, Lieutenant, Polish Army, (Fig. 6:5), was a Polish administrator responsible for 'signing off' PRC personnel upon their entry into civilian life. Working alongside British Army staff, and under the command of a British officer, he was billeted at Witley Camp until the last few Polish soldiers became civilianised.

When it was first conceived in 1946, "no final limit for the existence of the Polish Resettlement Corps was ever laid down." Up to December of that year a Polish serviceman was required to sign his 'PRC contract', which vaguely mentioned a commitment as "starting from the moment he signed up for the Agreed Duty": a position that was impossible to ratify. By February

Fig. 6:5 Lieutenant Szuta in 2010 on his 90th Birthday

55

1948, however, a woman enlisting in the PRC/ATS was asked whether she understood that her obligation was for a period of two years and that her 'PRC/ATS contract' could be terminated in writing, giving 15 days notice. Realising that "the existence of the Resettlement Corps might have been prolonged until a date two years after the last man had been enlisted, provided that he had not meanwhile been resettled into civilian life," Attlee's government reduced "the maximum period of enlistment to one year with effect from 12 March 1948 ... in order to hasten the final dissolution of the Corps." In this respect it seems that the government's first objective was to enrol the Polish servicemen and women in the PRC and the ATS/PRC respectively, then to stipulate the period of service, and finally to bring the existence of the Corps to a close by April 1949 as the last group of Polish soldiers were transferred from the Middle East in April 1948. The process of finally demobilising the PRC seemed to have stalled, however, as senior figures at Downing Street began to put pressure on the WO to probe the reasons for the "slowness of the run-down of the PRC."

In early January 1949 Emanuel Shinwell, Secretary of State for War, and George Isaacs, Minister of Labour and National Service (MoL and NS) called Major-General McLeod, Head of the Central Advisory Staff to the PRC, to a meeting. The purpose of the meeting, held on 17 January, was to establish "what steps could be taken to accelerate the run down" of the Corps. McLeod subsequently wrote to General Stanisław Kopański, Inspector General, PRC. In his letter of 21 January McLeod stated that there were "two factors militating against the run-down." The first was the "continued maintenance (cost) of Polish administrative staffs" to run the PRC. The second dealt with "the inclination of certain officers and warrant officers, to avoid civil employment, in order to enjoy … the higher … rates of pay and family allowances." He also revealed that the second point "can and will be dealt with by an intensification and stiffening-up of the attitude of the Anglo-Polish tribunals which deal with the so-called persistent refusers." McLeod asked Kopański to "re-examine establishments," including the Pay and Record Office at Witley. He wanted to "eliminate as far as possible the younger and more able-bodied personnel now employed on administrative duties, and substitute in their place elderly and less physically fit individuals who cannot be placed so easily in civilian employment."

The run down of the Corps came to a head on 28 April when the *Polish Forces Official Committee* accepted the recommendation of the *Select Committee on Estimates* to terminate the PRC by 30 September 1949. This meant that on the following day, 1 October, all Polish WO employees at Witley Camp, residing with their families at Tweedsmuir, became civilians. As such they were allowed to continue to stay with their wives and children at Tweedsmuir because the camp had been reclassified as a Families Camp on 15 November 1948.

A problem arose, however, when the WO realised in late 1949 that, by some clerical oversight, ***dependants*** had also been allowed to settle in the camp. Thus in October 1949 the WO found itself in the untenable position of being responsible for a large group of 'Tweedsmuir civilians', namely ex-PRC personnel who were demobilised at the end of September, their wives and children, as well as a group of dependants who were inexplicably residing there. For the WO this situation became difficult because at the time there was a policy in place, which stated that the NAB was responsible for dependants. However, the NAB argued that policy was being followed because in looking after the dependants at Tweedsmuir the WO was acting as the agent for the Assistance Board (Fig. 6:6).

> 3. Commands are requested to ensure that a clear distinction is drawn between "families camps" and "dependants camps". The War Department are responsible for the accommodation of Polish families whereas the Assistance Board are now responsible for the arrangements for the accommodation of dependants; as the Assistance Board are not at present in a position to arrange for the initial accommodation of these dependants, it has been agreed that the War Department will do this on an agency basis on behalf of the Assistance Board. The "dependants camps" will be handed over to the Assistance Board or some special organisation nominated by them as soon as practicable.

• Fig. 6:6

Besides, the WO was also of the opinion that as civilians, the ex-PRC servicemen were now in a position to seek civilian employment and that the process of looking for a job should be facilitated by the NAB or the Ministry of Labour.

Although the WO had tried in the past to encourage the NAB to take over the administration of Tweedsmuir Camp, the Board repeatedly refused to accept any responsibility. In 1949, however, the WO tried to approach the NAB again, this time through Lieutenant-Colonel HG Harborne, OBE, at the Aftermath Liaison Section - PRC / PLF Affairs. On 7 October, Harborne wrote a churlish letter to a Mr W Walton at the NAB. Among other issues Harborne explained that "Tweedsmuir is the families camp for the Civilianised Polish Staff of the PRC; the heads of the 90 family groups in WO civilian employment (at the Pay and Record Office) will gradually become redundant and so available for placing" in work, and that "among the above are about 12 oldish persons who are really only distant relations or hangers-on." He continued his letter to Walton by revealing that the Aftermath Liaison Section was "aware that you have refused to take over this camp as a hostel but we now desire to get rid of the 'bodies' ... by the end of this year (1949) or earlier." In the last few paragraphs, Harborne declared that "we should be very grateful if you could solve the problem for us." In return Walton expressed his opinion that "the problem" was for MoL and NS to solve and not for the NAB. The MoL and NS, however, also refused to accept responsibility for Tweedsmuir because they too did not see it as "our problem."

> PLF: Polish Land Forces

The WO had to act, responding in no uncertain terms to the letters it received from the NAB and MoL. In what was arguably the most influential communique that determined Tweedsmuir Camp's future, on 14 November 1949 the Officer Commanding (no name available) Laurentide Camp, Witley, informed the Board's Regional Controller in London that the WO had issued instructions to close Tweedsmuir by 31 December 1949, and that "all residents are being served with notices to vacate their quarters in the camp." The letter, which eventually stimulated interested parties into action, was brief and to the point. The NAB, however, responded by resisting to be pressed into action, choosing instead to "let the next move come from the War Office."

Although the notice to quit Tweedsmuir Camp was an enormous psychological blow to the Polish families living there, it was also a pivotal moment for them. Before the WO could make its "next move" the Tweedsmuir family heads formed a pressure group to oppose the notice, arguing that they did not seek to remain in the camp long-term but should be given time to reappraise their circumstances and to be given a fair hearing. They met early one evening in November 1949 in the Community Centre to discuss an intelligent strategy. To this end they looked to the *Stowarzyszenie Polskich Kombatantów* (Polish Ex-Combatants Association), Witley which, on 18 November, wrote a two page letter in broken English to the NAB, outlining the reasons why Tweedsmuir should not be closed immediately. Having explained the situation as perceived by the Polish civilian population of Tweedsmuir, the Combatants Association wrote, "… we Branch 107 of Polish Combatants Association submit to you kindly this question and appeal to you on behalf of these people for favourable consideration of the question and positive decision of this problem."

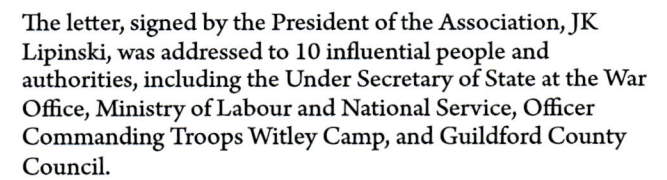

• Fig. 6:7

The letter, signed by the President of the Association, JK Lipinski, was addressed to 10 influential people and authorities, including the Under Secretary of State at the War Office, Ministry of Labour and National Service, Officer Commanding Troops Witley Camp, and Guildford County Council.

"Without wishing to appear unhelpful" administrators at the NAB continued to argue that they did "not regard the housing of these people as our job" but they did accept that the matter was "becoming one of urgency." To alleviate this and similar problems nationally, by the mid 1950s local housing authorities accepted responsibility for Polish families and dependants living in military camps as candidates for affordable housing. It is within this context that Hambledon Rural District Council was prevailed upon to take over the administration of Tweedsmuir Camp and run it as a civilian 'Housing Estate'. The Tweedsmuir Camp "hut dwellers", as the council referred to the camp's population, were permitted to stay on for the time being until their situation was clarified. This took a further 9 years.

Chapter 7

Family Life and Domesticity

• Culvert, which was once part of the water management system comprising a stone bridge and a canal

Life in the camp for the early Polish inhabitants tended to be a mixture of the familiar Polish culture and the newly found British culture. Although their 'Polishness' drove their way of life, their 'Englishness' was beginning to make its mark.

As stated in Chapter 2, Tweedsmuir was originally built to accommodate around 1,000 Canadian military servicemen in transit; there were no women on the site during the war years. The men were housed in 'T' shaped dormitories built from timber (one is highlighted in the portion of the aerial photograph in Fig. 7:1). However, the introduction of family groups after the war presented many difficulties because the camp was never envisaged as a living area for women and children. For instance, providing privacy when going to the lavatory in a camp originally built for 1,000 men.

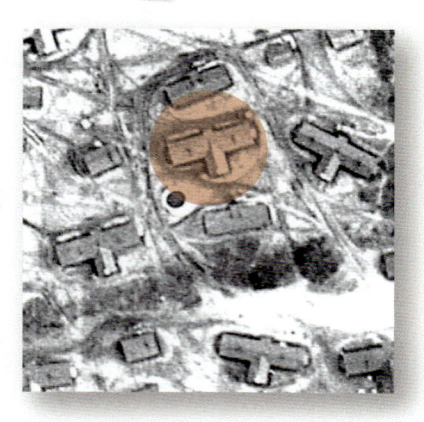

• Fig. 7:1

The first families to be accommodated at Tweedsmuir were the wives and children of family heads who were employed by the War Office at Witley Camp. The list of Tweedsmuir families started in 1947, comprising men, women and children who had either been reunited there after the war, or who had married in Surrey, notably St Edmunds Catholic Church in Godalming (Fig. 7:2). The process of Tweedsmuir becoming a Families Camp continued until it was officially recognised as such on 15 November 1948 (see page 57). The official civilian phase of family life at Tweedsmuir started on 1 October 1949, one day after the disbandment of the PRC at a national level.

The most appropriate accommodation for families were the timber dormitories, comprising running water and some storage. Once the dormitories had been allocated, other buildings, such as Nissen huts, which were used in Tweedsmuir for storage or as a hospital during the war, and timber buildings that served as offices until February 1947, had to be assigned to families. Of course, Nissen huts and offices had no running water, so in these instances the art of 'self-sufficiency' was exercised. In one case, for example, water was plumbed in by way of a hose. In another, a galvanised bucket stored water after being collected from a nearby stand pipe.

Fig. 7:2 Sergeant M Rogalski with his wife Stanisława on their wedding day outside St Edmund's Catholic Church in 1947

The exact process of how the barracks were assigned to each family is unclear. However, in some cases, a shortage of accommodation resulted in childless couples sharing a living space with another couple until new quarters became available. In some instances the living space was divided by a grey army blanket hung from a line.

Having been assigned barracks, families were given the opportunity to buy army furniture from a depository, using "pocket money" given to them by the WO who acted as "agents" for the NAB. Cupboards, tables, chairs, and heavy, steel framed beds with horsehair mattresses were available for a nominal fee as were cups, dishes, saucepans cutlery, and bedding. It appears that each family was also given the opportunity to buy a *Primus* stove on which to cook (Fig. 7:3). These and similar items were used to set up a home, and

Fig. 7:3 Mugs, dessert plates and a Primus stove from the 1950s

although they were of a utilitarian design, they satisfied the basic domestic needs. However, a home is more than a collection of functional items; it is also a social space just as much concerned with security and a feeling of wellbeing as it is with eating and sleeping. These 'higher' needs were difficult to satisfy because items such as photographs and keepsakes of loved ones were often lost during the war.

It seems that every family owned holy pictures and crucifixes, which were either hung on walls or stood on sideboards. Holy icons (see Fig. 7:4 for example) became extremely important to these families and perhaps provided the only direct link to home in Poland. The Catholic faith also enabled these people to make sense of exile, displacement and loss.

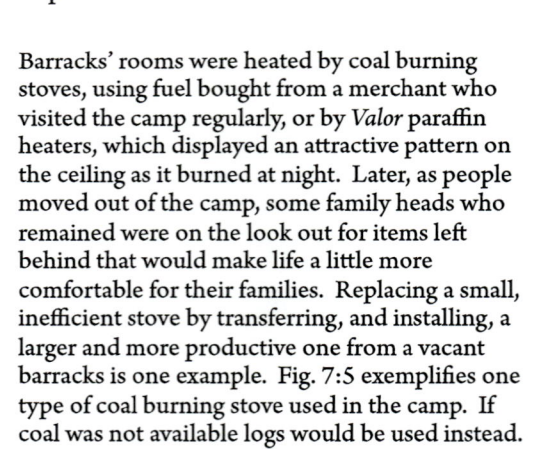

- **Fig. 7:4** Black Madonna Częstochowa. This picture hung on a bedroom wall at No. 39 Tweedsmuir

Barracks' rooms were heated by coal burning stoves, using fuel bought from a merchant who visited the camp regularly, or by *Valor* paraffin heaters, which displayed an attractive pattern on the ceiling as it burned at night. Later, as people moved out of the camp, some family heads who remained were on the look out for items left behind that would make life a little more comfortable for their families. Replacing a small, inefficient stove by transferring, and installing, a larger and more productive one from a vacant barracks is one example. Fig. 7:5 exemplifies one type of coal burning stove used in the camp. If coal was not available logs would be used instead.

As a military camp built for 1,000 men, bathing and showering facilities in Tweedsmuir were communal. Heavy, black tarpaulin screens provided privacy, and duckboards on a cold concrete floor a modicum of comfort. Men, women and older children used these facilities at any one time. Anyone who wanted to bathe or shower had to leave their barracks with their washing accoutrements under their arms and walk to the bathhouse. Although acceptable in the summer, this practice was less so

- **Fig. 7:5**

in winter when the nights had drawn in and the temperature had dropped to near freezing. With small children these arrangements were not recommended and so they were often bathed in tin baths within the barracks. The water was heated in saucepans on the *Primus* and poured into the bath until there was enough for a successful wash.

Adjoining the bathhouse was a laundry room which contained large earthenware sinks and wooden draining boards. The laundry was hand washed using a preferred washing powder such as *Tide, Lux* or *Persil* and a washboard (see Fig. 7:6). There were no labour saving devices available except a mangle. The washing was hung to dry on permanent frames in an adjoining room, which was well heated. It was often the laundry room that provided an opportunity to meet with others and exchange news. Such social exchanges became important as the community had little contact with the outside world and because individuals relied on each other to keep up with events.

• Fig. 7:6

Toilets were communal and housed in latrines. While the cubicles used by men and older boys did not have doors, women's cubicles did have them. Given that the camp was first built for men, it seems likely that the doors were fitted before the arrival of wives married to Polish servicemen. Each toilet seat comprised two banana shaped pieces of beech fixed to the pan and so the seats were not hinged. While the toilet pans and urinals in the latrines were made from white earthenware, the cisterns were made of cast iron, painted green (the aged lid in Fig. 7:7 is the top of such a cistern). Of course younger children used 'potties' kept in the barracks.

• Fig. 7:7

The comment has often been made that Polish individuals in the camp dressed well. Smart clothes were important to the families because they contributed to the rebuilding of self-esteem, something that was important to maintain during their early years in Britain. It was also a sign of their proud heritage and familial background.

Fig. 7:8 A Christening at Tweedsmuir Camp. All of the people in this photograph moved away from the Thursley / Elstead area after the camp closed

For special occasions, such as Christenings (Fig. 7:8), clothes were bought in shops in Guildford or Godalming. For those who did not posses a car or motorbike, shopping trips were difficult as the bus stop for the route number 24 was on the bend of the old A3 outside Thursley village (Fig. 7:9). Any purchases had to be carried to the camp through Thursley village on the return journey. The bus stop was removed in 2002.

Fig. 7:9

During the period of rationing the acquisition of food was difficult. When the camp first opened to accommodate PRC families, Barbara Januszewska and her husband leased South Park Farm in Hazelmere. The lease was for 14 years with the option of buying it later. She brought cabbages grown on her farm to the camp for grating and pickling. The pickled cabbage was then sold at the camp's NAAFI to Polish PRC personnel at Tweedsmuir, and from other camps in the area (eg Witley and Jasper), to make a Polish/Lithuanian dish known as 'bigos', or hunter's stew. The stew usually comprises any ingredient that suits the palate, such as beef, bacon and mushrooms.

Later on, many of the camp's inhabitants used their initiative keeping poultry such as hens, geese and ducks for fresh meat and eggs. Also, it was common practice to pluck the down from the breast of a goose and use the soft feathers to fill pillows and quilts. The head of one family, Mr Adamek, was even able to purchase, at a farmers' market in Guildford, goats and calves, which he fattened up for sale (Fig. 7:10). According to his daughter and son their family never seemed to have had a shortage of yoghurt or milk.

• Fig. 7:10

Some families grew vegetables in their small gardens adjoining the barracks. Potatoes, runner beans and beetroot were commonly grown. Others, however, had ornamental gardens, comprising flowers and ferns grown for pleasure. Many of the adults were also ardent mushroom pickers and could often be seen foraging for them in the woods around the camp. The mushrooms would be used to make mushroom soup or dried for seasoning dishes.

Clearly, not all the food requirements could be grown in a small garden. Fruit and cheeses, for instance, were bought from the General Store in Thursley owned by Mr Karn. (The store has since been converted to private accommodation and an extension added: Fig. 7:11.) He also visited the camp, usually on a Saturday afternoon, to sell produce such as bread, chocolates, lemonade and ice

• Fig. 7:11

65

cream from his van. A local dairy delivered one or two daily pints of milk, which could not be left on the step for long as blue tits were very adept at peeling back the bottle top to drink the layer of cream. Other salesmen also visited the camp selling items out of suitcases across the doorstep, such as English-Polish dictionaries, Polish books, nylons, underwear and holy pictures.

As elsewhere in Britain there were few, if any, labour saving devices in the camp, and women had to work hard to maintain cleanliness in the barracks. Floors were covered with Linoleum, which was polished regularly, and rugs were frequently beaten outdoors.

As Tweedsmuir Camp was set deep in the Surrey countryside, all kinds of flying, crawling and walking insects would take up residence during the summer months in the barracks. Stings and swellings from insect bites were part and parcel of living there.

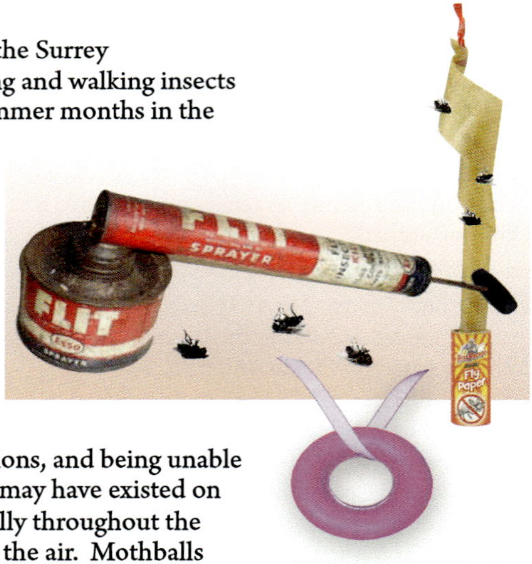

The two most widely used types of pest control against the common housefly were *Flit* and *Flypaper*. Although an effective insecticide, *Flit* caused an uncomfortable irritation at the back of the throat. Without the presence of 'Health and Safety' regulations, and being unable to read any English warning labels that may have existed on tins and containers, *Flit* was used liberally throughout the barracks: in corners, under beds and in the air. Mothballs and purple coloured naphthaline ring wardrobe hangers were used widely to control the infestation of moth larvae. When the community met for Mass on a Sunday morning, the naphthalene vapour in the air tended to clear the nose and sting the eyes.

• **Fig. 7:12** Pest control

After the introduction of the National Health Service (NHS) on 5 July 1948, it appears that all the occupants of Tweedsmuir registered with Doctor Lascelles whose practice was in Elstead. A district nurse, who lived in Thursley, visited families to monitor the health of children in particular, and to offer advice on their wellbeing. Families also registered with a dentist in Godalming who had a surgery close to The Pepperpot and recommended the use of particular brands of toothpaste (Fig. 7:13).

Radios and televisions were a luxury and not many families could afford them. However, people visited those with televisions and watched programmes together. The coronation of Queen Elizabeth II was one event watched by both children and adults on a tiny screen in a darkened room. Children also watched weekly programmes such as *Lenny the Lion*, and *Champion the Wonder Horse* (Fig. 7:14). In summer, when windows were open, popular songs of the time could be heard coming from the barracks. Flanagan and Allen's *Maybe its because I'm a Londoner*, was a hit in 1947 but was frequently heard playing in the 1950s.

• Fig. 7:13

There was no 'street lighting' in the camp and so people tended to stay in their barracks during darkness. However, if a journey could not be avoided, as for example going to Christmas Eve Mass, torches were used to light the way. As people made their tentative way outside, beams of light could be seen penetrating the darkness, reminiscent of wartime searchlights. If the torch was switched off accidentally the individual was left in absolute darkness, becoming apprehensive at taking a step forward.

The camp could never satisfy the physical or emotional needs of the Polish community for long, as it represented a transitional time between life in Poland and life abroad in England. For many the army units to which these people belonged during the war were surrogate families and to leave them was little more than a leap in the dark but leave them they did. The camp, by its very nature, was an imitation of home. It represented change rather than permanence and everyone knew that sooner rather than later the camp would be disbanded and the people moved on. Marriages represented the future and the birth of children signified hope and perhaps these were the first signs of a process of assimilation into British society.

• Fig. 7:14

67

Chapter 8

Patterns of Employment

Foundations of the Guardhouse built in the summer of 1943 next to the Thursley Road entrance

Finding work was not a particularly easy task. Eleven years would pass before the strict requirements put into place to control the employment of personnel from the Polish ex-Forces were revoked, making life then somewhat easier.

The ability of Polish individuals in Tweedsmuir Camp to earn a living would determine their economic independence, and their long-term purchasing capability. Through economic independence families could start to determine their own destiny, and a long-term purchasing capability gave them the opportunities to ultimately achieve something better than they had at Tweedsmuir Camp.

Although some of the early inhabitants of Tweedsmuir were employed as administrators by the War Office at Witley Camp, they were ill-prepared for civilian employment in administration because their English language skills were weak. This difficulty was usually avoided by taking work and positions where the ability to speak and/or write in English was not a strict requirement.

In the areas surrounding Tweedsmuir Camp arable agriculture, light engineering, and the building industry provided the best opportunities for work. Among those who secured such local employment were heads of families with expertise that was both unsuitable and unacceptable in Britain under the PRC scheme. For example, a policeman (Fig.8:1), steam locomotive driver and a livestock manager had to take work that required a change of career.

Whatever job the Polish individuals found it was important for the British authorities to keep a record of their movements and work patterns from the beginning. As an enlistee of the PRC or ATS/PRC, the movement of each serviceman and woman was recorded in a *Soldier's Service and Pay Book - Army book 64/Part 1* (Fig. 8:2). It was standard issue to all personnel in the British Army.

- **Fig. 8:1** Edward Modzelan in 1956. He was a policeman in Warsaw before the Second World War started

The Soldier's Service Book included the enlistee's army number, and personal details such as surname, christian name and date of birth, a record of privileged leave and travel, as well as the person's medical history. There was also a section which recorded the soldier's Next of Kin and the soldier's Will.

The transition into British civilian society for each Polish individual was marked by the provision of a *Certificate of Registration* under the Aliens Order Act of 1920 (Fig. 8:3). The actual procedure of issuing the certificate depended upon whether the individual was a man or woman, and whether or not he or she had served in the Polish Forces during the war.

- **Fig. 8:2**

For a Polish woman who had not been in the Polish Forces during the war, the issue of the certificate was almost immediate. Maria Modzelan, for example, married Edward in Italy, arrived in the United Kingdom (UK)

- **Fig. 8:3**

69

on 2 October 1946, one month before her husband (who was serving in the Polish II Corps), and was issued with a Certificate of Registration 28 days later on 30 October (Fig.8:4).

For a Polish woman who had served in one of the Polish Forces during the war, the certificate was issued when she was discharged. Stanisława Rogalska, for instance, enlisted in the ATS/PRC on 6 February 1947, married, received her *Certificate of Registration* on 21 January 1948 and was discharged one day later.

A Polish man who had enlisted in the PRC upon his arrival in the United Kingdom had to accept work which was sought for him by the MoL and NS. He was then allowed a period of anything between one and three months to decide whether or not the job suited him. During this period, the WO would have "released" the individual "from the PRC to the reserve" (Fig. 8:5).

• **Fig. 8:4**

• **Fig. 8:5** Taken from page 2 of the Certificate of Registration. Certificate Holder: Mikołaj Rogalski

This meant that if the individual, or his employer, felt the job was unsuitable, the individual was required to go back into the PRC. If, on the other hand, the work was agreeable to both the employer and employee the person would have been "finally discharged" (Fig. 8:6) and the *Certificate of Registration* issued.

> FINALLY DISCHARGED from the Polish Resettlement Corps on 6.12.48 (H.O. Circular No. 237/47). Not to engage in any business, profession or occupation for reward, otherwise than in the service of an employer, without the permission of the Home Office. (Aliens (Employment) Polish Resettlement Forces) Order, 1948).

Fig. 8:6 Taken from page 3 of the Certificate of Registration. Certificate Holder: Mikołaj Rogalski

Polish women, however, irrespective of whether or not they had served in the Polish Army during WWII, were prohibited from taking employment without the permission of the MoL and NS, and the Home Office (Fig.8:7).

The issue of this certificate does not entitle the holder to establish herself as to seek employment in the United Kingdom.

Not to take or continue in employment without permission of the M of L & NS nor to engage in any other occupation for reward or business or profession without the permission of the Home Office Aliens (Employment) (Allied Forces) Order 1946.

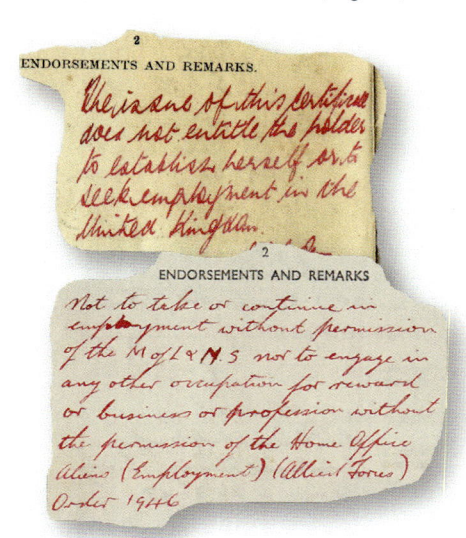

This restriction was lifted in 1953.

Fig. 8:7

The *Certificate of Registration* had to be carried at all times and produced at the local police station every time the individual moved house or became newly employed. A registration fee of 1 shilling (5 new pence) was charged to the holder when the document was first submitted to the police (Fig. 8:8), with strict penalties if the owner failed to comply with the 6 point notice printed on the back cover of the certificate (Fig. 8:9). These conditions had to be observed until 1960 when a new *Aliens Order Act* abolished the central register, exempting individuals from registering with the police. When the new Act came into force on New Year's Day 1961, the notice was crossed out in blue ink by a police officer.

• Fig. 8:8

However, it should be noted that all foreign nationals were expected to follow the same procedures when applying for a job or permission to remain in the UK; it was not something pertinent to ex-PRC personnel alone.

As mentioned in the first 3 paragraphs of this chapter, most ex-PRC men accepted work and positions where speaking and/or writing in English was not a strict requirement. In effect this led them to seek manual jobs. In this respect, there were many companies that accepted these men for work. For example, *Nutbourne Brickworks Ltd*, was a major construction employer, instrumental in the post war regeneration of local areas such as Farncombe, Godalming and Milford.

• Fig. 8:9

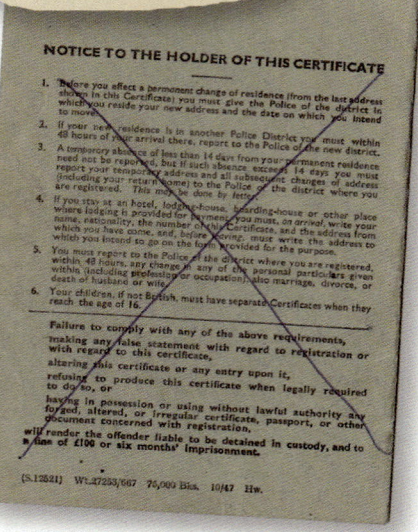

72

The Brickworks no longer exists (Fig. 8:10). The site has been bought by Millgate Homes of Berkshire. Millgate has recently applied for planning permission to transform the old brickworks into, what has been described as a grand "country seat." The company has signed an agreement not to identify the prospective purchaser but has revealed it is someone "famous for being very English." At the time of writing, the rumour is that Prince William could be the mystery buyer, looking to develop a new £20m estate.

• **Fig. 8:10** Nutbourne Brickworks Ltd photographed in October 2001. At the time the site was awaiting redevelopment

The *Weyburn Engineering Company* in Elstead was another renowned local employer (Fig. 8:11). At its height the company employed nearly 400 men, some of whom came from Tweedsmuir Camp.

• **Fig. 8:11** The Weyburn Engineering Company, which made camshafts, was closed in 2008 by its new American owners Federal Mogul

Reginald Foster Dagnall founded *RFD Inflatables Ltd* just after WWI. The company made, among other products, dinghies and barrage balloons. The original factory at Godalming burnt down in 1936 (Fig. 8:12) and was rebuilt in 1954, providing good work opportunities for both men and women. Dymitr Czertko was one head of family at Tweedsmuir who managed to secure a job at *RFD Inflatables*. When the newly built factory had been completed, RFD diversified into the manufacture of emergency equipment for the emerging civil aviation industry, as well as constructing lifejackets and life rafts for the RAF.

• **Fig. 8:12**

Individuals who had bought motorbikes or cars could pursue work some distance from the camp. In 1955 for example, after six years of local employment, Jan Kot secured night work, as a member of the maintenance team, with H J Heinz Ltd in North London. He travelled to work every Sunday on his motor cycle, lodged with a Polish family during the week, and returned to Tweedsmuir on the Friday morning. When the camp closed, his family moved to Thursley village. Jan Kot, however, continued to work at Heinz until 1981.

Tweedsmuir men also managed to secure employment at Dennis Brothers Engineering Ltd in Guildford, and Vokes Ltd Henley Park, Guildford who made industrial filters.

• **Fig. 8:13** Polish women picking and packing cabbages

From 1949 to 1957 *Secretts* of Milford employed women from the camp as land-girls who picked and packed crops (Fig. 8:13). As 1949 was only 3 years after the enforcement of the Aliens (Employment) (Allied Forces) Order that restricted them from engaging in work without the authorisation from either the MoL and NS or the Home Office, and 4 years before the restriction was lifted, it is highly likely that the women had sought permission to work.

Transport to and from work invariably involved a lift on the back of a *Secretts'* lorry, which would arrive daily through the Dye House entrance to the south of the camp, stopping along the camp's main road to allow the Polish workers to board, or alight, and leave through the western entrance in Thursley Road. Some women who remained in the local area worked at *Secretts* until 1969.

During school holidays children accompanied their mothers and would play in the fields as the women worked. Health and Safety was not a formal issue in those days, but luckily no accidents have been recorded from that time. Spinach, potatoes, sweet corn and tomatoes were typical crops. The women would pick the produce and bring it to collection points, which were dotted around the fields. It would then be loaded onto horse drawn carts and taken for processing at the grading and packing plant, from where it was dispatched for sale. Work finished at five o'clock, when a lorry was made available for the return journey. One perk of working for *Secretts* was the annual 'works outing'. The company provided a coach, which would arrive at Tweedsmuir Camp and take the employees to a show or pantomime in London.

Women from Tweedsmuir Camp were also employed as land-girls by both David Lloyd George's estate in Churt to pick strawberries, and by Barbara Januszewska and her husband at South Park Farm in Hazelmere, which concentrated on growing vegetables. Some of the most influential Polish dignitaries visited and stayed at South Park Farm, among them General Anders as shown in Fig. 8:14.

• **Fig. 8:14** General Anders being greeted by Barbara Januszewska's son, Krzyś, at South Park Farm

75

Chapter 9

Cultural Life

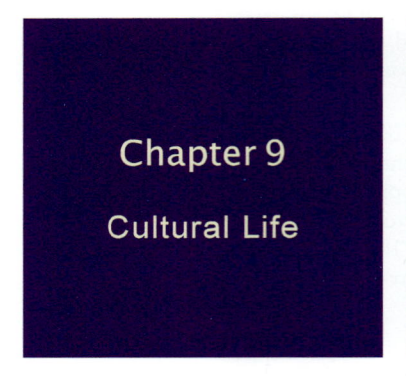

Remaining foundations of the Officers' Mess in the southern part of Tweedsmuir Camp

> Cultural life in Tweedsmuir Camp centred mainly around religion, national events, Polish traditions such as *Śmigus Dyngus*, and the printed word in Polish. Some effort was also made to form links with the local British community.

To all intents and purposes, the Polish community in Tweedsmuir was isolated physically and socially from the English community. Not only was the camp set in woodland, 600 metres from Thursley village, but the language barrier prevented meaningful social interaction. In this respect, the Polish ex-servicemen who married English women had an advantage over their fellow countrymen who married Polish women.

In their isolation the individuals in Tweedsmuir continued to practise their Polish customs, which became very important in maintaining their Polish heritage in a 'British' camp. Moreover, children of Polish parents were immersed solely in Polish culture, which further distanced them from the camp's surrounding communities. Their first language was Polish, as were their attitudes: a phenomenon that would not change until they entered a British school at the age of five. Conversely, children born into a mixed marriage, where the father was Polish and the mother English, had less of a culture shock as their first language at home was English, and therefore their sensibilities were arguably more in line with the British community outside the camp. However, as illustrated by Fig. 9:1, children from mixed parental backgrounds were able to absorb Polish traditions and culture.

The vast majority of the Polish community were Catholics. A small number, however, were Lutherans. Whereas observers of the Catholic faith worshipped in a timber built chapel at Tweedsmuir Camp (Fig. 9:2), Lutheran worshippers attended services at St. Michael and All Angels Church in Thursley. Consequently, the availability of numerous photographs which record only Catholic events in Tweedsmuir Camp give a biased view of the religious makeup of the people of Tweedsmuir, and add to the historical complexity concerning the understanding of cultural life in the camp.

- **Fig. 9:1** Maggie Lee (maiden name was Adamek; mother was English) wearing a traditional Polish costume

The Catholic priest at Tweedsmuir was Father Józef Bystry who, like many of his parishioners, arrived in Britain from Italy with the Polish Army. He was not only the spiritual leader, but an advisor, mentor and friend to the members of his congregation. To many of the people he was a link between them and the British authorities as his adequate command of the English language allowed him to communicate with British officials.

- **Fig. 9:2** Father Józef Bystry preaching to the Catholic Tweedsmuir Community at Sunday morning Mass

The Catholic calendar is full of religious festivals such as Corpus Christi, which is usually celebrated with a procession. It allowed the Tweedsmuir community to unite in prayer with other Polish ex- servicemen and women who lived in Algonquin and Laurentide Camps near Witley and in barracks at Dunsfold Aerodrome. The Polish Catholics accommodated in these camps hired coaches which brought them to Tweedsmuir to participate in the occasion (Fig. 9:3) because Tweedsmuir was regarded as the hub of Polish culture in the area.

In the week leading up to Corpus Christi field altars were constructed and erected throughout the camp, which acted as focal points for prayer. During the procession each altar was visited in turn, where prayers would be said. The procession had a specific order, which usually started with the camp's elder, carrying a large crucifix at its head, followed by two rows of altar boys dressed in red and white Albs, ringing bells. Then, two rows of girls wearing white dresses sprinkled flower petals to make a scented path on which Father Bystry would walk, carrying the Blessed Sacrament. A 'gold' baldachin (or 'canopy of state') carried by four adults signified the priest's authority as he clasped the Blessed Sacrament with both hands and presented it to the congregation whilst they processed (Fig. 9:4).

- **Fig. 9:3** Highlighted in the background is one of the coaches that brought members of the Catholic faith to Tweedsmuir for the Corpus Christi procession in 1954

Apart from Sunday Mass the Chapel was the setting for special celebrations, such as First Holy Communion. This is a very important occasion in a Catholic child's life and so parents made every effort to

- **Fig. 9:4**

78

ensure that their son or daughter was well dressed. The boys wore dark formal suits with short trousers and white socks, whilst the girls were dressed in delicate white dresses (Fig.9:5). Each child received a picture of The Last Supper, signed by Father Bystry, to commemorate the occasion (Fig.9:6).

In Poland Christmas is celebrated on Christmas Eve with the family. In Polish the celebration is called a *Wigilia* from the Latin *Vigilia*, meaning 'Eve of a Feast', and is sometimes referred to as a vigil. The Wigilia begins with prayers followed by the sharing of a blessed wafer (*opłatek*), during which family members wish each other good health and happiness for the coming year. After this a special meal is served, including beetroot soup (*barszcz*), pasta parcels (*pierogi*) filled with mushrooms, or mashed potato seasoned with soft cheese, sliced onion, salt and pepper, and fish dishes. Meat is not eaten on this day as it is traditionally a day of fasting and abstinence.

Polish customs call for the Christmas Eve meal to be served at dusk when the first evening star appears in the sky, and with a Christmas tree adorned with candles, baubles and cotton wool snow. After the vigil, Tweedsmuir families made their way in the dark to the Community Centre for collective celebration. When Father Christmas arrived to distribute presents he was accompanied by an angel, which represented virtue, and a devil which symbolised evil (Fig. 9:7). The characters of Father Christmas, the angel and the devil were played by adults who took turns to dress up in costumes prepared in secret during the months leading up to December. Today, the inclusion of evil in whatever

• Fig. 9:5

• Fig. 9:6

• Fig. 9:7

79

guise, is no longer seen as a traditional necessity.

On Palm Sunday each family attended Mass carrying sprigs of Pussy Willow tied in a bunch, a tradition that continues to this day. The following weekend, on Easter Saturday, small baskets containing bread, salt, Polish sausage and decorated eggs (*pisanki*) were taken to be blessed by Father Bystry and then eaten on Easter Sunday after Mass. Easter celebrations continued into Easter Monday with an unusual tradition known as *Śmigus Dyngus*. It was the day when teenage boys endeavoured to soak teenage girls with water.

• Fig. 9:8

The Community Centre was a large hall containing a piano, billiard table and easy chairs. This was the place where people met over a drink and a cigarette to spend a relaxing time together. Occasionally, dances were organised for the community, which allowed for fun and enjoyment.

The camp's community was able to keep abreast of international and national events by reading the Polish Daily and the Soldiers Daily (*Dziennik Polski i Dziennik Żołnierza* - Fig. 9:9). The Polish Daily was first published in London in 1940, and the Soldiers Daily for army personnel in Scotland. The two papers merged in 1944. It was only in the early part of the 1990s that the Soldiers Daily became a subtitle. The newspaper focused on articles and information that were of interest to the exiled community and not only did it contain a political editorial, but included a correspondents' section, advertisements and announcements. The editorial staff was drawn from the exiled community based in London, and so it understood well the needs and anxieties of its readership.

• Fig. 9:9

News was also shared during informal gatherings. For example, groups of 'Polish Tweedsmuirians' often met at the

80

Moat on Thursley Road, near Elstead. A summer treat was to have a picnic there at the water's edge where the adults sat on blankets with food and drink, whilst the children splashed about in the water. Such occasions would be a chance to enjoy the Surrey countryside, rest, exchange news, gossip and a laugh. The space around the Moat was a different place to what it is today. During the 1950s it was more of a recreational location where swimming, boating and car parking up to the water's edge were allowed.

Apart from religious festivals, Polish National Days were also celebrated. These focussed on the political history of Poland and were deemed important enough to be celebrated by Polish people everywhere. On the Sunday closest to May 3, for example, the community celebrated the birth of the Polish-Lithuanian Constitution, which was ratified on 3 May 1791. It was a chance to wear traditional costumes (Fig.9:10) and sing Polish songs.

• Fig. 9:10

Although the Tweedsmuir community was isolated geographically and linguistically, there were occasions when mixing with the English community was possible. For example, on 5 November parents and children would make their way to Thursley Village Green for Guy Fawkes' night. Seeing the the Roman candles, Catherine wheels and rockets, as well as the huge bonfire, was a wonder to the Polish people, although it is fairly certain that few of them understood the significance of this spectacle in Britain's history. There were also occasions when children were invited to Christmas parties at Thursley Village Hall. There they would join in, as best they could, singing English Carols, and pulling Christmas crackers for the first time before eating treats such as ice cream and jelly.

Chapter 10

Children and Schooling

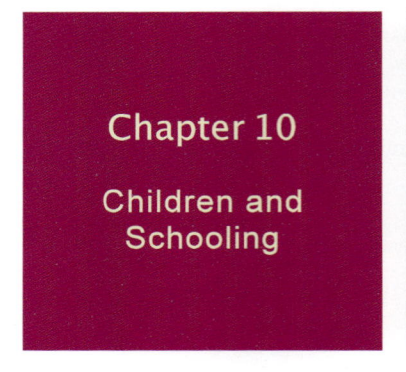

- A 19th Century horseshoe embankment, which trapped water from the water management canal

> The parents of Tweedsmuir Camp invested heavily in their children. The education of both boys and girls was of paramount importance so they were encouraged to achieve the highest standards they could.

The demography of the Polish population which lived temporarily in Tweedsmuir Camp changed rapidly between 1947 and 1954. Soon after their arrival, personnel of the 501 Basic Unit were reunited with their families, comprising wives and children, and their dependants who, during the war, had been placed in safe havens such as those mentioned in Chapter 5. As the children were born in Poland they had little, if any, knowledge of the English language. The priority for the British Government in this respect was not just to educate the heads of each family about British culture, but to provide an education for the children, enabling them to adapt more readily to a British way of life. To this end, as a direct consequence of passing the *Polish Resettlement Act* in 1947, the *Committee for the Education of Poles in Great Britain* (hereafter called the Committee) was formed, which became responsible for the education of Polish children in 20 nursery schools, 12 primary schools and 5 boarding schools. Each of the schools was located on the site of former military service camps, such as Diddington, now in Cambridgeshire, then in

Huntingtonshire (Fig.10:1), and Stowell Park in Gloucestershire (Fig. 10:2). In fact, the Diddington site was large enough to accommodate not just a school, but No. 6 Polish Field Hospital and a resettlement camp. Originally both Diddington and Stowell Park camps were built on private land to accommodate American Allied Forces during WWII.

In the months immediately after the war, Elizabeth Hopkins (maiden name Zimna) and Janusz Gąsiorowski were two young Polish students living in Tweedsmuir who benefited from the Committee's endeavours. While Elizabeth went to Merrow Grange Independent School in Guildford, Janusz attended school at Diddington Camp. As a boarder, he returned to Tweedsmuir during the school holidays. Janusz explained that he was taught in Polish as a lower school student, but in English when he reached the upper school. He subsequently achieved the required grades to complete his studies and became a dentist. Elizabeth finished her education at Cardiff University, qualifying as a pharmacist. They were two of the 1,549 Polish students who secured grants from the Committee to attend university.

• Fig. 10:1

• Fig. 10:2

From late 1947 to 1954 the number of children born in Britain to parents who lived in Tweedsmuir had increased, adding to the small population of pre-school children who had arrived at the camp with their parents between 1948 and 1951. George Jopek, for example, was born in Tel Aviv.

His sister, however, was born in Tweedsmuir Camp in 1954. By the time George started Thursley Primary School in 1956 the Committee was no longer functioning as it had ceased to exist on 30 September 1954. As the Jopek family (Fig. 10:3) emigrated to the United States of America in 1958, George and his sister finished their education in America where his name was changed from Jerry (Jurek) to George after King George VI who had died at Sandringham House in 1952.

Fig. 10:3 George Jopek, his mother, father and sister at George's First Holy Communion in Tweedsmuir Camp chapel

The vast majority of Tweedsmuir children who were born in Britain before the inauguration of the NHS in July 1948 were born in No. 6 Polish Field Hospital, Diddington. Many of the women who gave birth at Diddington would later describe the conditions at the hospital as very difficult. One said that she saw rats searching for food on the floor of the paediatric ward. Children born after July 1948 were mainly delivered at St Luke's Hospital in Warren Road, Guildford (Fig. 10:4) where conditions were superior to those at Diddington.

Tweedsmuir parents placed great emphasis on the education of their children. Those parents, having started on a professional career in Poland that was interrupted by the war, projected their ambitions onto their children, expecting them to follow a route that provided opportunities and a future. Parents who had received a basic education in some of the more rural eastern areas in pre-war Poland seemed to have responded to the 'mind broadening' experiences of the 1940s and the various educational opportunities that Britain offered.

Fig. 10:4 St Luke's Hospital, Warren Road, Guildford in 2002, awaiting redevelopment

The education of children born to Tweedsmuir parents started with the camp's kindergarten, which comprised one large barracks room. Maria Obara (Fig. 10:5) was the lead teacher. She had trained in Poland and arrived in Britain as a member of the Polish community. The curriculum was based on Polish custom and culture, and the development of Polish as the children's first language. Children's physical activities centred around playing with British made toys that included a steel framed seesaw, a rocking horse and puzzles. Along both side walls of the kindergarten were cots (Fig. 10:6) in which the children slept during the quiet hour between one and two in the afternoon.

Tweedsmuir Camp was surrounded by woodland, which provided wonderful resources for the children to enjoy. During the summer months Mrs Obara planned long walks in the fresh air. The children were barely visible above the bracken as they snaked along in pairs holding hands. When the right conditions prevailed the group would sit in a clearing or meadow, listening to Polish stories told by Mrs Obara.

One big advantage for mothers with children old enough to attend kindergarten was that it gave them the freedom to find employment, the earnings from which, supplemented their family's income.

When the children reached school age Surrey County Council was faced with two challenges. The first was to find places for the children at the local primary schools. It was the Council's policy to distribute numbers evenly in schools throughout the local area, hence places were made available at Churt, Elstead, Tilford and Thursley primary schools. The second challenge was to provide coaches for the journey to and from school except Thursley because of its close proximity to Tweedsmuir Camp.

• **Fig. 10:5** Maria Obara, top right, standing next to Father J Bystry

• **Fig. 10:6**

The Committee was beginning to wind down by the time the first post-WWII Polish generation started to attend primary school. Consequently, the Polish hierarchy in Britain was anxious that the sons and daughters of Polish émigrés would not lose the culture and traditions they had learnt from their parents. This led to the creation of a nationwide Polish organisation, which was established in 1953 under the title of the Associated Education Board for Polish Subjects and Culture in Great Britain (*Komisja Nauczania Przedmiotów Ojczystych Przy Radzie Kultury Oświatowiej Zjedoczenia Polskiego W Wielkej Brytanii*).

In 1954 the organisation became the supporting agency of the *Saturday morning Polish School* programme, whose function was to teach Polish children about their heritage. The scheme was adopted by the Tweedsmuir Polish community in the same year, and Józef Modzelan was one of the first students to be enroled. His report (Figs.10:7 and 10:8) shows the four key subjects deemed to have been important: Religion, Polish language (the spoken word, the written word and the printed word), Polish history and Polish geography.

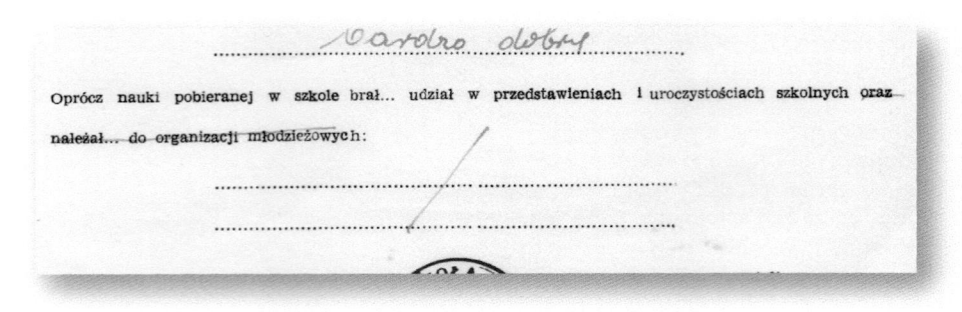

• Fig. 10:7

The portion of Józef's report in Fig. 10:7 also shows that children were expected to take part in extra curricular activities such as performances, school festivals and to belong to organisations such as the Polish Guides or Scouts.

Today the organisation has a much more succinct title: Polish Education Association (*Polska Macierz Szkolna*). It continues

KOMISJA NAUCZANIA PRZEDMIOTÓW OJCZYSTYCH PRZY RADZIE KULT. OŚWIATOWEJ
ZJEDNOCZENIA POLSKIEGO W WIELKIEJ BRYTANII.

SZKOŁA NAUCZANIA PRZEDMIOTÓW OJCZYSTYCH

w ...... *Tweedsmuir* ......

utrzymana staraniem Koła P.M.S. w ...*Koła Rodzicielskiego , S.P.K.*...

ZAŚWIADCZENIE

...*Józef Modrzelan*... ur. 4.10. 1947 r.

w ...*Diddington*... uczęszczał... w roku szkolnym 1954./5. na lekcje przedmiotów ojczystych i wykazał... postępy:

RELIGIA: ...*Bardzo dobry*...

JĘZYK POLSKI: na poziomie ...*początkowym*...
   a) w mowie ...*dobry*...
   b) w czytaniu ...*bardzo dobry*...
   c) w pisaniu ...*bardzo dobry*...

HISTORIA POLSKI: na poziomie ...*początkowym*...
   ogólna ocena ...*dobry*...

GEOGRAFIA POLSKI: na poziomie ...*początkowym*...
   ogólna ocena ...*dobry*...

Roczny program szkoły obejmował 180 godzin lekcyjnych z czego uczeń opuścił 20 godzin.

Zachowaniem swym, pilnością i starannością w nauce przedmiotów ojczystych, zasłużył... na ogólną ocenę: ...*bardzo dobry*...

Oprócz nauki pobieranej w szkole brał... udział w przedstawieniach i uroczystościach szkolnych oraz należał... do organizacji młodzieżowych:

Podpisy opiekunów szkoły: Podpisy kierownika i nauczycieli:

Tweedsmuir dnia 24.9. 1955.

• Fig. 10:8

to support established Saturday morning Polish Schools, while having strong links to the curriculum of English schools, which gives Polish children the opportunity to learn for example, about natural science and world history, and to study Polish as a language at GCSE, AS and A2 levels.

The teachers and children of the present day Saturday morning Polish School at Milford (Fig. 10:9) played an enthusiastic part in the *Tweedsmuir Camp Exhibition* project. Their work is reproduced in this publication. As in the 1950s, teachers at the postwar Saturday morning schools give of their time freely. Milford Polish school is also fortunate to have highly qualified professionals as staff. The Director, for example, has a Doctorate in Materials Science.

• Fig. 10:9

When Tweedsmuir Camp ceased to exist in 1959-60, the children of parents who had decided to stay in the surrounding area attended secondary schools such as Keys Cross before it became known as Waverley Abbey, Church of England (Aided) School, and Rodborough Hill before it became Rodborough Technology College.

However, the educational and cultural needs of Tweedsmuir children was little understood by the local primary schools. The language barrier was a distinct disadvantage in the classroom for both teachers and children and so the subjects the Polish children excelled at were those that did not require a good understanding of English, such as Maths, Art and Physical Education. The children's social development also suffered as they had to adjust to a different culture. In this instance Polish parents could help little as they themselves had limited understanding of the British way of life.

Very few English books, annuals or comics were available in the camp, and even if there had been the Polish children would have had difficulty understanding them. Equally, literature, such as Black Beauty and Heidi, which may have been available at the homes of British children, were not readily accessible in the camp. This meant that the literacy skills of Tweedsmuir children were limited until they entered primary school.

Bizarre at it may seem, school dinners were a concern for a few of the Polish children as they had been brought up on a Polish diet and were therefore unfamiliar with British food, which however nutritious, just did not suit the palate. Fish and chips, and swede for instance, were particularly disliked by some Tweedsmuir children.

Immediately after the introduction of the NHS, an inoculation programme against diseases such as diphtheria was begun at Tweedsmuir (Fig. 10:10). The vaccine was administered by Polish doctors at the same Medical Inspection Room (MIR) as had been used by the Lorne Scots regiment during the war.

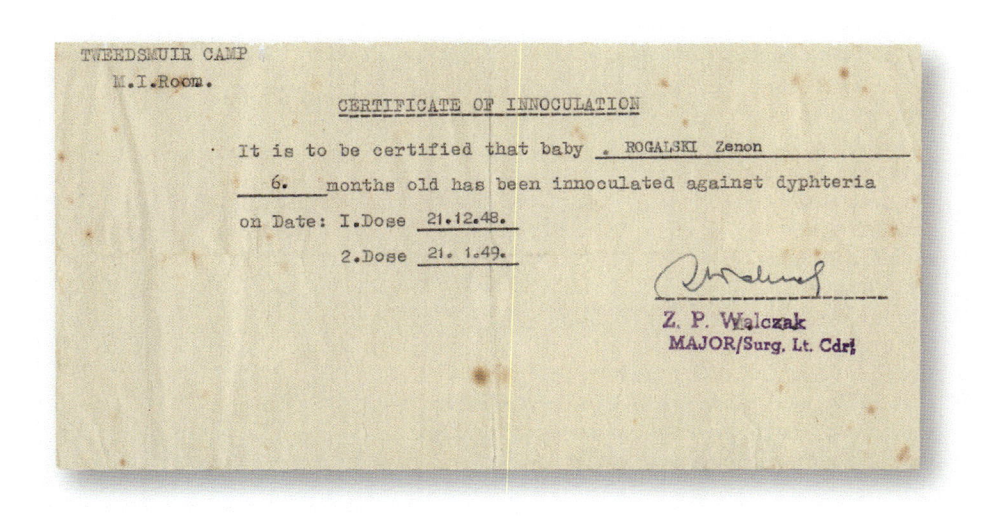

- **Fig. 10:10** Certificate of inoculation signed by Surgeon, Major Z Walczak. Note the misspelling of 'inoculation' and 'diphtheria'

Vaccines for some of the other diseases such as polio and measles had not yet been developed. No parent likes to see their children suffer through illness, therefore the two diseases most dreaded by Polish parents were polio and tuberculosis (TB).

Tweedsmuir Camp seemed a safe and secure place where children were left to play outside with a minimum of supervision. They played in groups and looked out for each other and so parents were not unduly worried.

Imaginative play became a central theme of the children's amusement. For instance, Zbigniew Lis recalls how groups of boys defoliated bracken stalks, and threw them through the air like spears.

However, the difficult circumstances in the camp did not mean that children were completely short of toys and games. Toys were bought on shopping trips to Godalming and Guildford. Dinky toys, clockwork as well as electric train sets, and plastic moulded vehicles, which were introduced in the early 1950s, were the desire of many boys. Girls tended to play with plastic moulded tea sets, prams and dolls some of which were lifelike.

During the winter months popular indoor pastimes included colouring books, spinning tops, jigsaws and alphabet building blocks (Fig. 10:11).

• Fig. 10:11

Many children received tricycles, chariots and peddle cars for Christmas, which were usually reserved for playing outdoors in the summer. *Tri-ang* toys (Fig.10:12) seemed popular as the company had led the way in the 1950s with the manufacture of all manner of indoor and outdoor toys. There were also instances where a father used his skills to manufacture a go-cart from planks of wood and recycled pram wheels.

In the late 1950s barracks lay empty as families moved out, creating exciting playgrounds for the children of families who were still waiting to relocate. In the same way as children in cities played in the ruins of bomb sites after the war, Tweedsmuir children played in the disused barracks. Some would climb in through broken windows to investigate whatever remained inside. Others managed to climb onto barracks' roofs to remove and throw felt roof tiles like *frisbies*.

It was not uncommon to find spent rifle cartridges on the ground, which made a whistling sound when thrown through the air. Sometimes the odd live bullet was found, which also stimulated the adventurous spirit of boys. Two other military items played with were gas masks, and white silk parachutes of a type that reduced the fall of a flare to the ground. Wearing a WWII gas mask for thirty seconds left one with a hatred for the smell of rubber for the rest of one's life. However, tying a stone to the six strings hanging from a small parachute, throwing the assembly into the air and watching it descend towards the ground left one with a sense of calm satisfaction.

• Fig. 10:12

91

Chapter 11

Demise of Tweedsmuir Camp

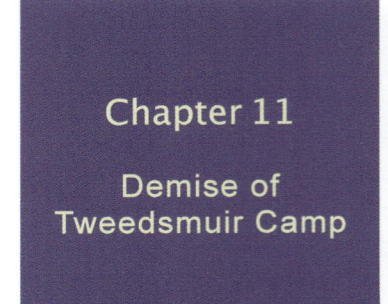

- Concrete crossovers adjacent to the Thursley Road entrance. To the left stood the maintenance garage

The winding up of Tweedsmuir Camp was overseen by Hambledon Rural District Council who had run it as a civilian Housing Estate. The council wanted to close the camp by 30 September 1957, but it remained open for just over 2 years more.

The closure of Tweedsmuir Camp was conducted by Hambledon Rural District Council (HRDC), the forerunner of Waverley Borough Council. From the day HRDC took over the camp in the first few months of 1950, it ran it as a civilian Housing Estate because by then all of Tweedsmuir's Polish occupants had been demobilised from the army. Consequently the council's priority was to manage the process of closure by acting as agents of national policy.

Like other county councils HRDC relied heavily on the work of various committees, and the dissolution of Tweedsmuir was no different in that it was managed by a housing committee. Captain G Davies was its Chairman and Major-General W Cave-Browne Vice Chairman. Intriguingly, Cave-Browne was present at the meeting held on 19 March 1941 when the construction of Tweedsmuir was being discussed with the Canadian Corps Commanders at the War Office. Other members of the committee included such dignitaries as Commander R Slayter, Lady Midleton, Brigadier G Portman,

The Honourable Mrs B Loyd and The Reverend Stanley Hide. They met at the Council Offices in Bury Fields, Guildford, Surrey.

One of the very first decisions taken by HRDC was to dismantle unoccupied barracks, and rehouse some of the families in private accommodation as soon as they were able to. However, despite the speed with which the barracks were being pulled down, in May 1950 the contractors responsible were told they could not "dismantle all the huts for twelve months!" The reasons for the delay are not recorded but it would seem that at about this time the Ministry of Housing and Local Government (MoH and LG) were reviewing the national housing programme. Why this review was necessary and just how it affected HRDC's plans for rehousing the Polish people living in Tweedsmuir Camp can be extracted from national and local documents.

With a slim majority after the 1950 election, Attlee called for another ballot in October 1951 in an attempt to increase Labour's share of seats in the House of Commons. This time the Conservative Party triumphed to form the next government under Winston Churchill. The 1951 Conservative manifesto stated that under "the Socialists … waiting lists for council houses in many districts are longer now than they were five years ago." As a substantial number of Tweedsmuir Polish families had requested to be put onto HRDC's waiting list for a council (today affordable) house the reason why the dismantling of barracks at Tweedsmuir had been halted before the 1951 election may have been due to the council's lack of opportunities in providing these families with alternative accommodation.

Soon after the 1951 election, the HRDC housing committee received two letters which frustrated the speedy rehousing of Polish families living at Tweedsmuir. The first came from the former housing minister Harold Macmillan who became Prime Minister of Britain from 1957 to 1963. Macmillan urged "the use of bricks, particularly local bricks, in the construction of houses." It would seem that he was turning to the Housing section in the Conservative Manifesto, which identified the need to "revive the confidence of the Building Industry and greatly widen the scope for the independent builder." The second letter was sent by the Principal Regional Officer of the MoH and LG, "asking whether the council proposed to include Cornish Unit houses (prefabricated from precast concrete) in the 1953 or 1954" building programme. The housing committee appointed a sub-committee to investigate, and report back their findings on the use of Cornish Units. On 8 December 1952, one year after the sub-committee was appointed, it tabled its findings saying "that in their opinion there was nothing to recommend the erection of these houses in preference to traditionally built houses apart from the speed of erection." As a consequence it was "resolved that such houses be not built in the Hambledon Rural District." However, building houses from traditional materials would require more careful planning over a longer period of time. Thus had HRDC dismantled the barracks in Tweedsmuir with no suitable alternative accommodation for the Polish families to move into, the rehousing programme would have been in further chaos. Moreover, since Tweedsmuir was one of four such sites in the district, the problem of relocating all the Polish families would have become unmanageable. It wasn't until the end of 1952 and the beginning of 1953 that HRDC sought a solution to the problem in earnest.

The housing committee discussed many sites upon which to erect traditional houses. Clappers Meadow in Alfold, Portsmouth Road in Milford and Roke Lane in Witley were three such locations. Two other sites were the "Nursery site, Elstead" (as referred to by the housing committee) positioned between Ham Lane and the B3001 Milford Road, and the Springfield Estate situated directly opposite the junction of Ham Lane and Milford Road. It seems that the largest number of Tweedsmuir families who decided to settle in the local area chose to do so in Elstead; a smaller number chose Thursley or Milford.

At first several land owners were "unwilling [...] to sell to the council, by agreement, land in the vicinity of the Nursery site" and an adjoining estate called Elstead House. Finally, however, in 1953 HRDC purchased the site "at a negotiated price thus saving the need of a compulsory purchase order." A similar situation arose at Roke Lane, Witley, where the acquisition of land came to a temporary halt because of an objection from "the authorities of St. George's College

Preparatory School", which called for the housing committee to recommend that "a compulsory purchase order be made in respect of the reduced area of land now required."

According to council minutes, the MoH and LG authorised the demolition of Elstead House "in the interest of economy and increased housing accommodation." On 6 June 1954 the housing committee minuted that "on receipt of this authority, the work had been commenced." Other transactions regarding land in the locality of the Nursery site were less controversial. For instance, a successful meeting was held "between the Engineer and Surveyor, Mr Gocher, his solicitor and the Clerk upon the acquisition of the piece of land next to Elstead House Cottage and the suggested settlement by the District Valuer was accepted."

Notwithstanding the difficulties of acquiring land for redevelopment, the council agreed that "up to 25% of the Nursery site area should be allocated for private building." By 9 March 1953, a tentative layout plan had been "submitted by the Engineer and Surveyor ... which was agreed in principle subject to the acquisition of further land and to the access road being made under the *Private Street Works Act* to ensure that half the cost is borne by the owners of the private properties benefitting thereby."

Just as the HRDC was getting to grips with the whole question of rehousing the Polish families, it received a letter from the MoH and LG in early 1953, stating that "no further expenditure would be allowed upon the huts at Dunsfold Camp and the huts at Tweedsmuir Camp." Consequently this threw into disarray the council's original decision not to build Cornish Unit houses and its plans for housing expenditure, resulting in an urgent need to find appropriate sites on which houses could be built. Nevertheless, "after considerable discussion" the council "agreed that the letter be accepted and it was resolved to recommend that the occupants of the huts at Dunsfold Camp be rehoused in accordance with the policy already laid down and that the huts, as vacated, be demolished and that when the camp has been cleared, the same policy be applied to Laurentide Camp and to Tweedsmuir Camp. It was felt that to expedite this policy, some sites should be found whereon some non-traditional houses (Cornish Units) could be erected."

The absence of financial support for the upkeep of Tweedsmuir placed an enormous strain on the camp's infrastructure. After a heavy downpour the sewage pumps, situated at the lowest point of Tweedsmuir Camp, became increasingly clogged with silt brought down from the higher reaches of the site, causing them to stop working just as had happened during the Canadian tenure in the 1940s; except that in the 1940s the problem would have been resolved. The drains became blocked, toilets failed to flush and the living conditions were falling into a state of irreversible disrepair. Meanwhile the vacant barracks were being demolished as families moved out (Fig. 11:1).

- **Fig. 11:1** L to R, Ted Sysiak and friends. In the background stands the guardhouse built to the left of the Thursley Road entrance in 1943. In the middle-ground a contractor demolishing what was once the cinema

It remains unclear whether or not the "non-traditional houses" were ever built by HRDC. What is clear, however, is the speed with which the council responded. On the same date as it received authorisation for demolishing Elstead House, for example, the housing committee agreed names for the roads that were to be constructed on the Nursery site. The minute reads: "Upon consideration of recommendations from Elstead Parish Council it was resolved that the principal road to be constructed [...] be known as *Broomfield*, and that the cul-de-sac be known as *Hazelwood*."

Existing records reveal that the layout plans for each of the sites on which HRDC was planning to build houses continued to be revised until the housing committee agreed that the

96

number of houses proposed for construction satisfied demand. This in itself was quite an achievement as accommodation requirements varied from month to month. One consequence of this strategy was that the building programme had to be extended over several years.

The accommodation plans being prepared for the Tweedsmuir families had to fall into line with central government policy. On 24 August 1954 the housing committee discussed a memorandum it received from the MoH and LG, which asked for particulars that related to "the number of houses to be erected by the District Council during 1955 for the specific purpose of,

i. rehousing 'hut dwellers' (as the Polish families living in camps were called by the council), and
ii. replacement of category '5' (affordable) dwellings."

In response the council resolved to inform the Ministry that the estimate for these two purposes would be,

i. 50 and
ii. 40.

Three months later, on 8 November 1954, the Principal Regional Officer of the MoH and LG permitted the council to "let contracts for 90 houses."

The council's policy for rehousing the Polish families was that they "should be dispersed throughout the district so that each parish takes its share of the occupants from the hutments." The Clerk was instructed to discuss the problem with the Engineer "to ascertain the estimated flow of completions of council houses so that a broad policy of dispersal be based upon his report."

"An *Agreement and Schedule of Conditions of Building Contract* for constructing the final phase of Hazelwood and erecting houses thereon" was signed on 29 April 1959 between HRDC and Benjamin George Merriman of Churt, Surrey. Later that year, and towards the beginning of 1960, houses in Hazelwood were nearing completion and prepared for accommodation. Although the exact number of Tweedsmuir families who moved to Hazelwood has proved difficult to trace, the fact that a few did, shows that Tweedsmuir Camp existed as a post war Polish family housing estate beyond 30 September 1957: the date by which HRDC announced Tweedsmuir would close.

Despite Tweedsmuir Camp being run down, one or two families continued to live in the barracks. As agreed by the council in 1955, they were eventually relocated to other parishes in the district, including Thursley.

One of the very last acts of protest against the Soviet regime by the Polish people of Tweedsmuir before they moved away from the camp, manifested itself in a march on 22 April 1956 against the visit of Soviet leaders *Bulganin* and *Khrushchev* to London. The march, which included hundreds of ex-PRC soldiers from similar camps in Britain, was organised by the Polish Ex-Combatants Association. A hired coach took a party of twenty one adults from Tweedsmuir Camp to London (Fig. 11:2) and returned at the end of the day.

• Fig. 11:2

98

At the time of writing, it is just over 51 years since Tweedsmuir Camp ceased to exist. The site is becoming increasingly less easy to decipher as a place that once accommodated people from two different nations: Canadian and Polish. However, by making a study of a few articles tossed aside over half a century ago, it is at least possible to get some idea of the history of the people from the camp. Some of these articles are shown on this, and the next 2 pages.

Image No.	Description
85i	Mug used in the Officers' Mess
85ii	Part of a hinge from a military vehicle
85iii	Shard of reinforced glass from a Nissen hut
85iv	Long valve from a military vehicle's back wheel
85v	Double hook from the inside of an army issue wardrobe
85vi	2 Reinforcement rings from a tarpaulin shower curtain
85vii	12 mm thick key hole escutcheon plate, probably from the guardhouse
85viii	Reinforcing batten from a window blackout screen
85ix	Piece of felt roofing shingle

86i

86ii

86iii

86iv

86v

86vi

86vii

86viii

86ix

86x

Image No.	Description
86i	Fragment of an acetate record; commonly known as a '75'
86ii	Ladies open toe pantoffle shoe and heel tip
86iii	Glass medicine bottle. On its front is etched the word "POISON"
86iv	*Famel* Catarrh and throat pastels tin
86v	Remains of an army issue pocket knife
86vi	Double cream bottle top
86vii	Booth's gin cork top. Cork has perished since the top was last used
86viii	Hot water bottle stopper
86ix	2 *Garton's* H.P. sauce bottle stoppers
86x	Steel enamelled saucepan handle

Image No.	Description
87i - 87vii	Fragments of pottery from various locations at Tweedsmuir Camp

It would seem that by 1950 the Polish people of Tweedsmuir were becoming used to living in Britain. For example while illustrations 85i to 85ix encapsulate the camp's military phase, 86i to 86x, and 87i to 87vii typify the kind of products (mostly British) used by the Polish civilians. Despite living in barracks and Nissen huts, music, English fashion, alcohol and food were becoming part of their lifestyle.

Apparently, some of the Tweedsmuir civilians had been in possession of a wide range of pottery products from different parts of the world. For instance, 87i to 87iii are shards of British pottery. The 87iv piece, on the other hand, appears to have an Arabic-style calligraphy on its base. Image 87vi includes a Greek Key pattern, which was often incorporated in Italian design. Finally, inscribed on the underside of 87vii is the word 'Czechoslovakia'.

From this, is it possible to argue that 87iv to 87vii are the remains of ceramic-ware brought from abroad by the Polish people of Tweedsmuir and are a testament to the journey of individuals between 1939 and 1950?

Chapter 12

After Tweedsmuir Camp

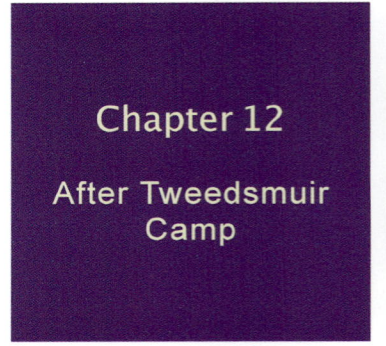

• Features of the water treatment plant remaining in the very south of Tweedsmuir Camp

The number of Polish people living in Tweedsmuir Camp fluctuated until 1956 when the number of families started to decline. The barracks were demolished between 1959 and 1960 and the site returned to the War Office.

In the final analysis, around 18% of the Tweedsmuir Polish families decided to remain in the local area after the camp closed, finding accommodation in, for example, Elstead, Milford and Thursley (Fig.12:1). Their religious needs were met when Canon Denis Hawkins, parish priest of St Edmund, King & Martyr, in Godalming made an agreement with Father Józef Bystry and Mateusz Czuchnicki, president of the Tweedsmuir Residents Association, that Holy Masses could be said in Polish at the church. The Polish families who had been accommodated at Algonquin Camp, Laurentide Camp and in the barracks at Dunsfold Aerodrome in the 1950s, and who had also decided to remain in the area, joined the Polish congregation of St Edmund. Together they built a new community under the guidance of Father

• **Fig. 12:1** Locations in Thursley (top) and Elstead (bottom) to which families from Tweedsmuir Camp relocated

102

Bystry and Mateusz Czuchnicki. This arrangement lasted for 26 years.

In 1985 a new catholic church was built at Milford and consecrated as St Joseph Roman Catholic Church. This became the new religious focal point for the Polish families in the area, and continues to be used by the present Polish community who share the church with the local English community.

• **Fig. 12:2** Celebrating Christmas at St Edmund, King and Martyr Church Hall in Godalming. Note the spelling of "Christmas"

It would seem that by the early to mid 1960s the Polish community at Milford was beginning to allow its 'Britishness' to surface as shown in Fig. 12:2. Flanked by British decorations on either side, the greeting above the stage reads "Happy Christmass" [sic] instead of the traditional Polish greeting, *Wesołych Świąt Bożego Narodzenia*. One intriguing feature in this photograph is that of the 58 people visible only 4 are young children. This is such a different scene to the one in the 1950s as shown in Fig. 12:3. Although it has proved difficult to establish precisely why so few children attended the Christmas festivities recorded in Fig. 12:2, two possible reasons are as follows.

Firstly, families with children had either emigrated or moved away from the area. Secondly, the children who were between 5 and 10 when living in Tweedsmuir Camp had become teenagers with a preference for participating in a culture that provided them with modern music, fashion and the excitement of revolutionary technologies such as the transistor radio. This is not to say that the second generation of 'Tweedsmuirians'

• **Fig. 12:3** Celebrating Christmas at Tweedsmuir Camp. The festivities focused on children receiving presents from the dominating figure of Santa Claus, and taking part in the Nativity play

lost their affection for Polish culture and heritage, but that they seem to have learnt how to manage being Polish in a British environment whilst respecting their parents' values.

A photograph that is worthy of inclusion at this point records the visit of Bishop Szczepan Wesoły to the Polish parish of Milford and Godalming in 1975 (Fig.12:4). With Father Bystry and Mateusz Czuchnicki on either side of the Bishop there is a suggestion of continuity within the community. Despite becoming increasingly integrated into British society, the local Polish community's desire to take part in the Bishop's visit illustrates the importance the parishioners placed on links to their Polish heritage. Again, as in Fig. 11:2, no children of school age are present in this photograph.

Fig. 12:4 Visit of Bishop Szczepan Wesoły who was assigned to the Polish community in Great Britain as Delegate of the Primate of Poland for Polish émigrés Abroad. Sitting to the Bishop's right is Mateusz Czuchnicki (former president of the Tweedsmuir Residents Association) and standing to the Bishop's left is Father Bystry

From the information available, just over 6% of the Tweedsmuir families emigrated to countries such as Australia, Switzerland and the United States of America; some as late as 1971. All have fond memories of living in Tweedsmuir by citing, for example, bicycle rides to Elstead, splashing about in the Moat on Thursley Road near Elstead and visiting Mr Karn's shop in Thursley. Krystyna Goryniewska, for instance, who now lives in New Jersey, USA, remembers buying Mars bars from Mr Karn's village store. For her the chocolate bar became a "most important item at the age of nine" and is "still one of my favourites." She remembers how one December she and members of her family were stopped on the Thursley Road by a policeman on a motorcycle as they dragged "a fir tree across the road to the camp for Christmas." Despite being "ticked off we managed to keep the tree." Hania Czarnecka-Borowska, who also lives in the USA, explains that she too has fond memories of the camp, vowing to return there on her next visit to England.

A little over three quarters of the Tweedsmuir population (76%), however, decided that London should be their new destination when the camp closed. In conversation with two *Tweedsmuir Camp Exhibition* participants who moved to London in the 1950s, the reason for choosing the capital was that it offered better opportunities for their children: schools, further education and jobs were in greater abundance. There is also evidence to suggest that families who relocated to London had done so because their heads had lived in large Polish cities before the start of the Second World War and hence preferred to live in an urban environment. For example, Edward Modzelan lived in the capital Warsaw, Mikołaj Rogalski in Tarnopol (today Tarnopil is in Ukraine) and Stanisław Szelegieniec in Katowice, a city in southern Poland. Although it would be incorrect to draw any firm conclusions from such a small sample, it is a plausible and relevant reason why some Tweedsmuir families relocated to London.

Picking an area in which to live was not a particularly difficult task as the suburbs chosen had already been populated by Polish people in the late 1940s and early 1950s. For Tweedsmuir families the preferred London suburbs for resettlement were Ealing, Chiswick and Clapham. A small number of families also made their way to Croydon and Slough. For the purpose of this publication the Polish parish of Clapham will be cited as an example of resettlement in London.

The Polish Clapham Parish in South West London was officially established on 15 May 1955, becoming the second largest Polish parish in the city (Fig. 12:5). The Tweedsmuir families who decided to live in this part of London were joining a community that had already formed links with Polish doctors and dentists, financial advisors, as well as solicitors who helped them to purchase anything from an

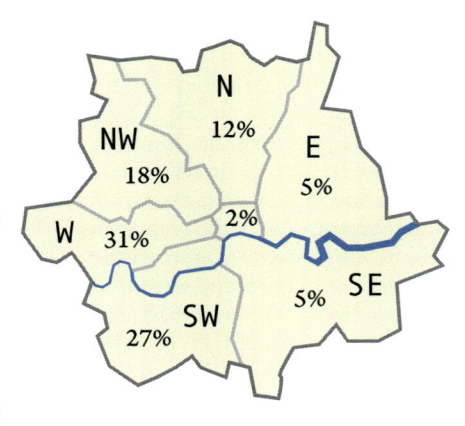

• **Fig. 12:5** Resettlement of Polish people in London after the closure of military camps

105

insurance policy to a house. It was not long before the 'Tweedsmuirians' were successfully integrated in the parish, being actively encouraged to do so by the parish priest Father Stanisław Cynar who, according to his parishioners, was a man with exceptional organisational and motivational skills.

Father Cynar had a special empathy with the servicemen and women who had served in the Polish II Corps, as he had been chaplain to various units and formations of the Corps. He arrived in Britain from Italy with the first wave of Polish Army units in the summer of 1946, worked briefly as a builder prior to purchasing a house in Clapham North. Before the official birth of the parish, in 1948 Father Cynar approached the Redemptionist Fathers at St Mary's Church , Clapham (Fig. 12:6), seeking permission to say Holy Mass there in Polish at 1.00 o'clock every Sunday afternoon. "Out of concern for the youth of the parish," as Mr S Wiśniowiecki wrote in a 1952 Clapham Polish Parish brochure, Father Cynar arranged alcohol-free social functions at St Mary's Hall around the corner from the church (Fig. 12:7). He was vice-chairman of the *Towarzystwo Przyjaciół Dzieci i Młodzieży* (The Association of Friends of Polish Children), which organised a Saturday morning Polish School, nursery school and boarding facilities for 45 boys who were students between the ages of 16 and 20 (Fig. 12:8). A similar arrangement was established for girls between the ages of 14 and 25 at a different building in the same road. In 1950, to the surprise of the parishes' English neighbours, Father Cynar led the first Polish Corpus Christi procession in Britain. The event prompted

• Fig. 12:6

• Fig. 12:7

• Fig. 12:8

the *Kominikat*, published by the *Gmina Polska Londyn-Południe* (Polish Community of South London) to write that "such a procession had not been seen in the streets of London for some 300 years." As an event the procession was soon repeated in other parishes, and camps like Tweedsmuir. Father Cynar's drive and ambitions attracted new parishioners, some of whom were families from the Tweedsmuir community who had moved to London in phases between late 1956 and 1958.

London provided opportunities to continue with familiar cultural traditions. For instance, Tweedsmuir children who had been born in the mid 1950s were too young to prepare for their First Holy Communion at the camp. The Polish parish of Clapham, however, gave them the opportunity to fulfil this obligation (Fig. 12:9), which was marked by issuing a commemorative certificate signed by Father Cynar (Fig. 12:10). Unlike at Tweedsmuir, however, there was a reception for all the participants afterwards at the Saturday morning Polish School.

The move to a large city necessitated finding both work and housing, and in this respect the benefits of networking in a tightly knit Polish community in London came into its own. For example, some of the Tweedsmuir men gained employment at a plastics factory in Croydon, which was established by a Polish ex-RAF fighter pilot, Karol Czajka, who changed his name to Charles Dugan-Chapman after the war. An injection moulded plastic doily and poppet beads were two products made by his factory. The beads, which snapped together to make necklaces and bracelets, were assembled at home by the wives of the men employed at Dugan-Chapman's factory. This was monotonous "piecework" for which the women were paid a fixed "piece rate" regardless of the time taken to assemble a large paper sack of beads.

• **Fig. 12:9** Wies Rogalski and his mother at his First Holy Communion reception in South West London

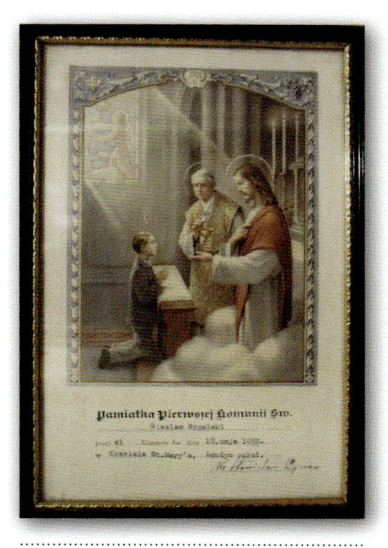

• **Fig. 12:10** Wies Rogalski's First Holy Communion certificate

The houses bought by the Tweedsmuir Camp families in south west London were a far cry from the barracks they had lived in since the end of the war. Fig. 12:11, for example, illustrates the Edwardian style properties Tweedsmuir families aspired to, and resettled in after 1957.

When the families arrived in the late 1950s there were few, if any, cars parked in the streets unlike today. The absence of vehicles must have been how the architects imagined the roads would always look like.

The incomparable shopping and recreational

Fig. 12:11 Streets in Clapham, London where Polish families from Tweedsmuir Camp bought houses

facilities (Fig. 12:12) were soon taken advantage of by the Tweedsmuir families who found themselves at the heart of a vibrant city.

• Fig. 12:12

As other military camps closed, the London Polish population increased in number. For example, numbers in the Polish Clapham parish swelled from 200 in 1948 to over 3,000 parishioners by 1966. The increase in parishioners encouraged Father Cynar to announce that it was his ambition to buy a building that could be developed into a Polish Catholic Centre. He understood that parishioners' commitment alone would not be enough to secure the capital required. He was, therefore, the first Polish parish priest to arrange a covenant scheme for his parishioners, which was a binding agreement that individuals would donate to the parish an agreed sum of money each week. By 1969 the Polish Clapham parish had raised enough to buy 'Hamilton House' in Balham High Street (Fig.12:13). It was renamed *Klub Orła Białego* (The White Eagle Club), and became

• Fig. 12:13

109

South West London's Polish cultural centre as well as a place for celebrating Holy Mass. In an attempt to maintain a national identity in exile that could be remembered by subsequent generations, a handful of Polish earth was placed in a small casket behind a large mirror inside the centre's entrance, and Second World War army insignias were hung on the walls of the function hall. The centre became an enormous success, hosting lavish dances, performances and other occasions. Some years later, in the spacious grounds to the back of The White Eagle Club, the community agreed to build St Anthony's Retirement Home for bereaved Polish people who would pay for their accommodation and food cooked on site.

In spite of the success of the White Eagle Club, Father Cynar was determined to buy the Polish Catholic parish its own church. Unfortunately his death in 1976 meant that it was his successor, Father Stanisław Świerczyński, who brought this proposal to a satisfactory conclusion when the United Reformed Church across the road from The White Eagle Club in Balham became available for purchase. Subsequently on 2 July 1978, the United Reformed Church was consecrated and renamed *Rzymsko-Katolicki Kościól Chrystusa Króla* (Christ The King Roman Catholic Church) (Fig. 12:14).

• **Fig. 12:14** Polish Roman Catholic church Christ The King

Like all Polish communities in Britain at that time, the Polish parish of Clapham was thriving on a unique kind of 'Polishness'; a 'Polishness' that was based on heroism, martyrology, pride of achievement and the Roman Catholic faith. This was encapsulated by living in a Polish world from Friday evening to Sunday evening, comprising events such as Holy Mass, attending social events at the White Eagle club, or at the alcohol free Polish students' club *Pod Parasolem* (Beneath the Parasol) in the basement of number 7 Cromwell Road SW7, joining the Polish Scouts or Guides, and playing football for *Grunwald FC*, an all Polish team in the Southern Area Sunday Football League. Adults often enjoyed lunch at the *Ognisko* (Polish Hearth Club) at 55 Exhibition Road, London, SW7.

As the Tweedsmuir families became more urbanised and their affluence grew they bought motorcars, which increased greatly their mobility. This gave them the freedom to travel and revisit old haunts in Surrey, including the site of Tweedsmuir. Moments that were particularly enjoyable included meeting old friends by the Moat in Elstead (Fig. 12:15).

Regrettably, by 1976 church numbers in the Polish parish of Clapham had dwindled as those who had been the backbone of the parish between 1948 and 1959 passed away, while the second generation had married and moved to more affordable locations. Eventually the reduction in the number of parishioners began to threaten the very existence of the parish. This scenario was being repeated in other Polish parishes in Great Britain. Two major events in post-war Poland would eventually influence the Polish communities in the UK.

• Fig. 12:15

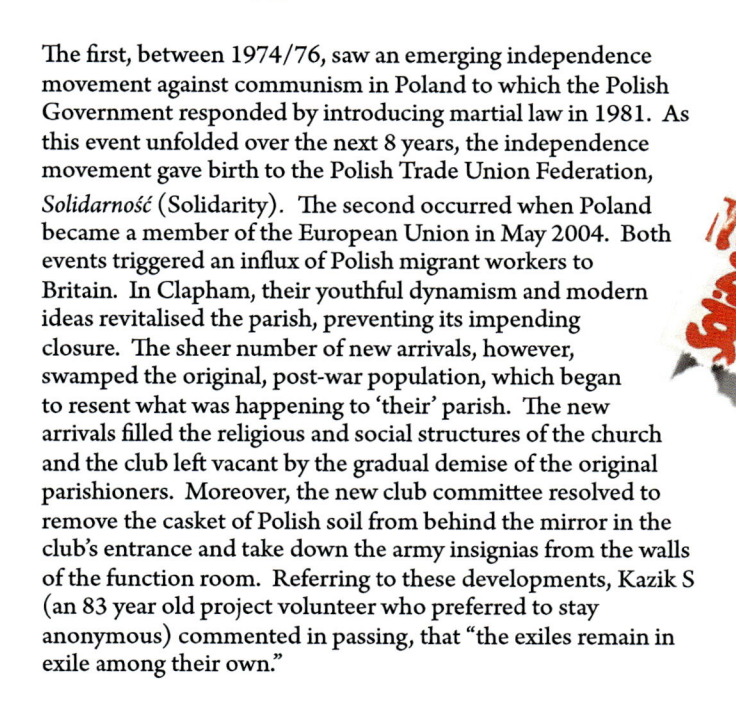

The first, between 1974/76, saw an emerging independence movement against communism in Poland to which the Polish Government responded by introducing martial law in 1981. As this event unfolded over the next 8 years, the independence movement gave birth to the Polish Trade Union Federation, *Solidarność* (Solidarity). The second occurred when Poland became a member of the European Union in May 2004. Both events triggered an influx of Polish migrant workers to Britain. In Clapham, their youthful dynamism and modern ideas revitalised the parish, preventing its impending closure. The sheer number of new arrivals, however, swamped the original, post-war population, which began to resent what was happening to 'their' parish. The new arrivals filled the religious and social structures of the church and the club left vacant by the gradual demise of the original parishioners. Moreover, the new club committee resolved to remove the casket of Polish soil from behind the mirror in the club's entrance and take down the army insignias from the walls of the function room. Referring to these developments, Kazik S (an 83 year old project volunteer who preferred to stay anonymous) commented in passing, that "the exiles remain in exile among their own."

Chapter 13

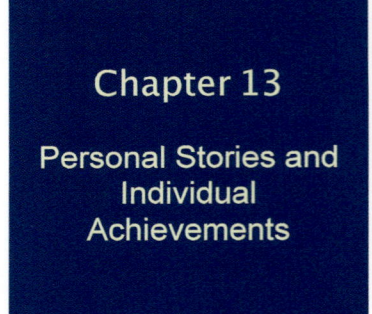

Personal Stories and Individual Achievements

• View of the parade ground and Tweedsmuir Camp's main road from under the water tower

The stories collated for this part of the booklet have been written either by individual volunteers, provided by volunteers in conversation, or from documents volunteered by surviving members of families who lived at Tweedsmuir Camp. Each account is presented under the volunteer's surname in alphabetical order.

Waldue Adamek's story:

Waldue, who lived at Tweedsmuir Camp with his mother, father and sister, is a Veteran of the Falkland's War.

I joined the Royal Navy on the 3 January 1966 at the age of fifteen. After 32 weeks of basic training I went to HMS Raleigh (named after Sir Walter Raleigh) in Torpoint Cornwall to await my first sea draft.

• **Fig. 13:1** On the day of his return from the Falkland's War, Waldue Adamek (left) is met by his father, Władysław Adamek

My first ship was HMS Carysfort, which was a WWII destroyer. I knew that I suffered from sea sickness but not how badly until I went to sea for the

112

first time. Whilst on the Carysfort we were involved with the Torrey Canyon incident. The Torrey Canyon was a supertanker that ran aground on rocks between Land's End and the Scilly Isles on the morning of Saturday 18 March 1967 and leaked 119,328 tonnes of crude oil into the Atlantic. After helping to plot the flow direction of the oil to ascertain the danger to the Cornish coastline, we sailed around the Cape to transit the Indian Ocean and onwards to visit the Pacific Islands.

I served on many ships, including HMS Belfast as part of the Reserve Ships Unit in the late 1960s. Today, HMS Belfast is moored on the River Thames and is open to the public as part of the Imperial War Museum.

I joined HMS Minerva (Fig. 13:2) little knowing that I would be in the south Atlantic in 1982 as part of the flotilla that set sail to protect the Falkland Islands.

Fig. 13:2 HMS Minerva, alongside Thorshavn, Faroes

We were lucky on the Minerva as we appeared to be in the right place at the right time. Soon after arriving at Bomb Alley (San Carlos Water - Fig. 13:3) we took over from the HMS Argonaut, which had been hit by two bombs that, luckily for them, did not explode but nevertheless had caused damage and death.

We were still in Bomb Ally when the surrender was signed on 14 June. Soon after we sailed to Goose

Fig. 13:3 San Carlos Water, Falkland Islands

113

Green and were able to stretch our legs on terra firma. We also got to speak to some of the locals and to see where they had been interned in the community centre during the conflict.

In early July we sailed home and, after a heroes' welcome, into Guzz (Devonport Naval Dockyard), Plymouth, where my father was awaiting my return along with other friends and family.

While we had some much needed leave the ship underwent a small refit before sailing back to the Falklands to take up guard ship duties for the Christmas period. Following patrol duties for a few days, we entered Port Stanley for the first time on New Year's Day where we were able to step ashore for a look round.

Edward Burczy's story:

In 1940 Edward was 3 years old. In the summer of that year he and his relatives, one of whom was his cousin Stanisława Burczy (later Rogalska who lived in Tweedsmuir Camp), were deported to one of the many USSR work camps. Today Ed lives with his wife in Arlington Heights, Chicago, USA. His story is a firsthand account of the trek he and his family made from Russia to the Middle East where his dad joined the Polish Army, and from where he and his mother were transported to the safe-havens of Tanganyika (now Tanzania), Mombasa and finally to Britain before emigrating to the United States of America.

It was midnight, wrote Eddie, very dark and bitterly cold. The Burczy family were told to leave their home by soldiers who wore long green overcoats to protect them from the frost. One soldier was kind as he allowed my mum to take a few extra things for me as I was very young.

- **Fig. 13:4** Ed Burczy, Arlington Heights, Christmas 1997

The whole family, that is my mum and dad, my four aunties my grandparents and I, were shipped out of Poland to Kazakhstan on cattle trucks. The trucks had narrow slits in their sides and an upper platform that you could reach by a ladder. I spent most of the journey on that platform, urinating as and when I had to. As I remember, the journey lasted for three days.

Soon after we arrived at our place of destination, granddad died and was buried in ground that was rock hard from the frost. I remember my dad cutting a tree trunk and making a cross for the grave.

My mum, it seems to me now, had a hard time with me as I was small and food was in short supply. She tried to find food such as eggs, bread and vegetables from sympathetic Russians with, I should add, some success. On other occasions my aunties gave me their food to eat. It was a very difficult time for us all: the loss of granddad, the cold, the misery and the total uncertainty of the whole situation must have played on their minds as they tried to keep afloat on a tide of fear.

When the Eastern Front opened, the Russians allowed the Poles to make their way out of the USSR. There was no transport provided. We had to make our own way to freedom. Dad made two sledges, one for mum, himself and me and one for my aunties. To this day, however, I remember only two of my aunties coming with us. It was much, much later, when I was 68, that I learnt the other two aunties had remained in Russia and were resettled in western Poland after the war.

I particularly remember the journey out of Russia as we made our way along narrow tracks through a dark tunnel of trees. My two aunties who came with us took turns pulling each other on their sledge. Occasionally a truck would drive by and dad would barter with the driver, offering him a pair of trousers, a jacket, sometimes money in return for a ride on the truck.

When we arrived at the point where the new Polish army was being formed, my dad enlisted. I remember him standing in front of me in his khaki uniform as his old clothes were burnt on a heap of other people's clothes. He was then transferred for training after which he travelled through southern Europe, the UK and eventually Normandy in France. I will never forget the time he waved to mum and me as he was transported off by truck. Both mum and I cried. I learnt later that dad served in 1 Armoured Division, 1 Polish Corps under General Maczek. My two aunties also joined the Polish army, leaving mum and me to comfort each other. Eventually my mum and I were shipped out to Africa. We spent various lengths of time in places like Tanganyika and finally Mombasa. The barracks in Mombasa were communal where both children and their mothers slept in the same large room.

Mombasa was heaven! There was a pier like the kind you might see in a film about *The Adventures of Tom Sawyer*. The sand was a pure golden yellow, soft and warm. I had an excellent time there. As soon as I woke up (usually around 5.00 or 6.00 in the morning) I'd put on a pair of shorts and a vest and go fishing. I made my own fishing line, which was tied to the end of a stick, and a weight I made from a piece of used toothpaste tube that I wrapped around the line. For those of us who remember, in those days toothpaste tubes were made from lead! I used to catch yellow and green coloured fish, which I threw back into the water. In the evenings I would go swimming with other kids in the camp.

I have taken the liberty of attaching a couple of pictures of the camps we stayed in. I hope you will be able to use them (Fig. 13:5).

My schooling in the camps was very basic. I remember older people, I'm not sure if they were teachers or not, teaching us Polish history and writing. Religion, however, was taught to us by a priest. But above everything else the best moments were when a letter would arrive from dad, and mum would read it to me.

When we arrived in the UK, I went to Polish school then,

• Fig. 13:5

afterwards, English school. This was in Liverpool, which, after East Africa, was cold and damp! By this time dad had returned from the war, landing in Liverpool where we all met up for the first time in 5 years.

In 1947 we moved to a camp in Chandler's Ford, Eastleigh just north of Southampton in England. My two aunties who had joined the Polish army at the same time as my dad, also came to live in England. Aunty Stasia settled in camp Tweedsmuir, Surrey before moving to London, Aunty Genia in a camp near Spondon, Derbyshire, and from there to Derby itself.

Mum, dad and I emigrated to America in 1951, settling in Chicago, Illinois. When I was older, I asked dad why he and mum decided to relocate to the USA. He explained that they saw no future living in a Nissen hut, which we had done for 4 years. The opportunities of setting up home in a completely new place was exciting, he said. He also told me that my mum's sister had been living in America since around 1910/12, and that it was because of her family's presence in the US that we were allowed to settle there.

Dad had set up a printing business in Chicago, which did very well. When he retired I took the business over and it went from strength to strength. Eventually I sold the firm and established a real estate partnership. Now I am also retired, both my mum and dad have died and I too have a family.

Elizabeth Hopkins' story:

Elizabeth Hopkins (maiden name Zimna - Fig.13:6) and her mother were one of the first Polish families to arrive at Tweedsmuir Camp from Poland. Elizabeth was 10 years old when she arrived at the camp. Her father was employed as WO staff at Witley Camp.

We arrived at Tweedsmuir Camp in 1948 and lived in a wooden hut that was divided into three rooms for three families, with no lavatory or bathroom. A round stove in the middle of the room was used for heating and cooking. My father was stationed nearby at Witley Camp. When the other two families moved to other huts in the camp we acquired their rooms. One was converted into a bedroom, and the other two into a lounge and a kitchen respectively.

• Fig. 13:6

There was a communal lavatory at the camp and a communal laundry, which was used once a week by the women. There were also communal bathing facilities, which were used by the women and men on different days. Although most children of school age were sent to boarding school, I did not want to go. As luck would have it my father, who was a winner in the European rowing championships in 1929, was able to get a grant for me to go to a private convent school through an old rowing club friend who worked at the Polish Embassy. At ten and a half years of age, with little previous schooling and no English, I travelled 2 hours each way to school, arriving back at 6.00 pm to chop wood and start meals for my mother who arrived later. When Witley Camp closed, my father spent the week working in a London factory, returning to Tweedsmuir for the weekend.

My grandfather had a bookbinding factory in Poland, which the Germans needed during the occupation of Poznań. He was also an entomologist with a collection of around 10,000 butterflies; all exhibited at his home in Poland. I remember German officers arriving to view the collection. He actually bred a moth that bears the name 'Zimnyi', which is latinized from Zimny (Fig.13:7).

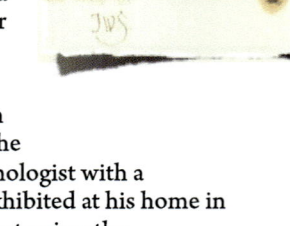

• Fig. 13:7

118

At the end of the war, as the Germans and Russians fought each other across Poznań, our home, including my grandfather's butterfly collection, were burnt to the ground. Despite this, not one member of our family lost their lives.

When a curfew was imposed my mother, while out, would dash into doorways to hide as troops sealed off the road and anyone caught would never be heard of again. Nevertheless, although these were frightening times, we had parties and visited friends.

The hospitals, trams, and cafés were *nür für deutche*, only for the Germans. When I developed a cyst I had no option but to go to a backstreet Polish doctor to have the pus removed with a syringe and without anaesthetic. I was held down and prevented from screaming so as not to alert the neighbours.

The Russian 'liberators' were no better than the Germans, as they raped women and shot Polish citizens. My father and others who were released from Siberia and enlisted in the Polish II Corps were declared enemies to the Russians and threatened to be shot if they returned to Poland. Hence my father smuggled us out by using all his savings to pay for false German passports, which enabled us to travel to England and eventually Tweedsmuir Camp.

When the time came for us to leave Tweedsmuir Camp I was 16 years of age with no qualifications. We arrived in London to rented accommodation and both my parents secured employment in factories. I completed my 'O' levels at night and arranged my own way into college for 'A' levels as my parents spoke little English.

After obtaining seven 'O' levels, and four 'A' levels in sciences, I studied Pharmacy at Cardiff University, where I met my husband. We returned to London and had two children, both of them girls who are bilingual, being able to speak in Polish and English. While one of my daughters is a dentist, the other is a pharmacist. I eventually became chief Pharmacist in a London hospital then went into business acquiring 7 pharmacies.

Apart from Pharmacy I was heavily involved with the Chiswick Saturday morning Polish School as Chair (first female *prezes,* or president), helping to keep the school open. It was important for the children to learn the true Polish history which was not taught in Poland under Russian occupation. I also worked tirelessly for other charities for which I received the Pope's Medal for Charity.

Recently I have been elected to a national committee to represent pharmacists, requiring me to negotiate at Government level. All my involvements have been enjoyable and rewarding.

Mike Kot's story:

Mike, his mother, father and two sisters were the only Polish people who moved to Thursley village after Tweedsmuir Camp closed. He is a Veteran of the Falklands Conflict and was involved in Middle East operations after the Iraq War (Desert Storm). Mike has had a distinguished career in the British Army.

I joined the army in 1969 after a few short-lived jobs such as a trainee chef, apprentice machinist, and forestry worker. The Army suited me to the extent that I made a career of it for 22 years, achieving the rank of Warrant Officer Class 2 (Quarter Master Sergeant Instructor), or 'Q' for short.

My army postings to British Army on the Rhine (BAOR) included 2 tours, Osnabrück and Willich, over a period of 8 years. I was also posted to various locations in the UK before becoming involved in construction and other projects in the Near and Middle East, Africa and Britain.

When the Falklands War started in April 1982, I was posted to the Islands with my troop where, among other duties, I became the official interpreter for 7 Polish deep sea fishermen who had 'jumped ship' in Port Stanley a few days before the Argentinean invasion of the Islands started.

Fig. 13:8 Mike Kot at Fox Bay, West Falklands

Fig. 13:9 Mike Kot on board the Queen Elizabeth II sailing for the Falkland Islands

After returning to the UK for a brief period, I was posted again to the Falkland Islands in 1985 for 6 months to reinforce the military infrastructure so that the Islands could be better protected in the future.

My final posting in the UK was at Bristol University Officer Training Corps (OTC) as Senior Instructor Combat Engineering, which includes training in a variety of tasks that facilitate the movement of support and friendly forces while impeding that of the enemy.

• **Fig. 13:10** WO Mike Kot (Retired) Front row, 3rd from right. The department was headed by a Lieutenant Colonel from the Kuwaiti Airforce (in uniform)

Having retired from the army in 1991, I went to live and work in the Middle East for 7 years. There I first worked as an explosives ordnance disposal operator post first Gulf War (Operation Desert Storm), then briefly as a Health and Safety manager on a major reconstruction project, and finally as a senior instructor (mechanical engineering) in an Arab military college (Fig. 13:10).

There are two events from my army career that are particularly satisfying. The first is the presentation of the Long Service and Good Conduct Medal presented to me by Lord Lieutenant of Chepstow in 1984 (Fig.13:11).

The second is receiving the General Officer Commanding Commendation "in the field" from Brigadier BC Jackman OBE MC, Commander 43 Infantry Brigade. I received this for exemplary conduct and professionalism at the scene of a serious fire involving a group of Ferret Scout Cars

• **Fig. 13:11**

at Limpley Stoke, near Bath, on 16 March 1990 (Fig 13:12). The second part of the citation reads: "Warrant Officer Class 2 Kot's prompt and courageous actions prevented the fire spreading removing the danger of further injuries to troops and the public."

• **Fig. 13:12**

Maggie Lee's story:

Maggie Lee (maiden name Adamek) is the sister of Waldue Adamek whose story began this chapter.

My mother was English and worked as a nurse at the King George V Sanatorium (for the Diseases of the Chest), Milford. The nurses were often invited to attend dances at Witley Camp and it was at one of these occasions that my father met his future wife and my mother.

Ours was one of three families in the camp with an English mother. At home, conversations between my parents tended to be in English hence my brother and I did not use the Polish language as much as the other children in the camp. On the other hand we did have the luxury of celebrating Christmas twice: as a Polish occasion on Christmas Eve and as an English occasion on Christmas Day.

• **Fig. 13:13** Maggie Lee with husband David at the wedding of their daughter, Geraldine, in the USA

We lived at number 2 Tweedsmuir Camp as it was the only vacant barracks on the site at the time. Soon after moving in, we discovered that the reason why the barracks remained empty was that people believed it to be haunted by a French-Canadian soldier who committed suicide in the sitting room. According to my mother, at one point she heard footsteps in the corridor of the barracks and said, "I know who you are and you don't frighten me." She heard nothing more from the ghost.

As my mother was English, she was able to help the Polish people at the camp by, for example, filling in forms, and acting as interpreter. She also ran the creche at Tweedsmuir Camp because she was a qualified nurse.

Despite having a job at RFD my dad used the farming skills he learnt in Poland to keep livestock in Tweedsmuir. Mum bought the cattle at Guildford market on dad's behalf, which were brought to the camp by Wally Ellis who farmed in Elstead. Once at Tweedsmuir dad put the calves out to pasture on land that, during WWII, was the Officer's lawn in front of the Officers' Mess. In the middle of the pasture was a Range Wardens security post, which was a square brick building with a stove and cold running water. Some of the calves mum bought would often develop scours (calf diarrhoea) as they were taken away from their mothers too soon. In this case dad would stay in the building tending to the calf until it could be left on its own. There was always resentment at dad keeping cattle on the old Officers' lawn because it had been earmarked as a recreational area. My mother, however, persuaded the housing office at Hambledon Rural District Council that part of the land could be fenced off for keeping cattle and goats.

Dad fed his cattle hay converted from grass he cut with a scythe at Thursley cemetery. In the afternoons my mother would walk into Thursley to turn the grass over to help it dry. When dad considered the hay to be ready, he brought it to the camp on the back of a trailer pulled by his van. His first van was a Ford 7, and the second an Austin 8. We used the milk from a Jersey cow called Topsy to make cream cheese and butter because, although the milk was very delicious, we were unable to sell it as we did not have the appropriate dairy facilities.

Today I have a great love for animals. However, when I was a little girl I wasn't allowed to keep cats or dogs as pets because dad considered them to have no value. Cattle, on the other hand, could be sold

• **Fig. 13:14** Maggie on Carousel

for a profit, and whilst rabbits could be reared for meat, chickens could be kept for both meat and eggs.

Our family had a strong link with the local English community. For instance, while I entered the Thursley Produce Competition for drawing and cake making, mum would enter produce grown in our Tweedsmuir garden.

When our family moved from Tweedsmuir in 1957, Wally Ellis helped by taking all our belongings by tractor and trailer to Hookley Lane in Elstead.

I became a legal secretary, joined the WRAF (Fig.13.15) as a typist and later became a shorthand typist. I eventually became the personal secretary to Group Captain Mason, an aviation pathologist at the Institute of Pathology and Tropical Medicine, RAF Halton.

I met my husband, David, who was an airman at RAF Northolt. After we married we moved to Lincoln where we bought our first home. Later, my husband went on to serve at the Headquarters Allied Forces Central Europe, which is part of the North Atlantic Treaty Organisation (NATO) forces at Brunssum, The Netherlands.

Our daughter Geraldine, whom we visit regularly, is married and lives in the United States of America.

• Fig. 13:15

Janina Lis' story:

Janina Lis (maiden name Popiel - Fig. 13:6), her husband Stanisław Lis and their son Zbigniew (Bish), arrived at Tweedsmuir Camp in 1947. Sergeant S. Lis was in the 501 Basic Unit, PRC and a member of staff at the Pay and Record Office, Witley Camp. Janina Lis has kindly agreed to share her story.

I was born in Kielce, approximately 115 kilometres south of Warsaw, in November 1927. When Nazi Germany invaded Poland I was 2 months short of my twelfth birthday.

Like millions of other families west of the Curzon Line in Poland at the time, we spent 4 years living under Germany's rule. In 1943, just before my 16 birthday, Nazi German soldiers kicked on the front door with their heels, demanding that our home be opened up and all the lights inside it turned on.

Everyone in the immediate vicinity was "rounded up" as one group, which was kept under constant guard. The fear I saw in people's eyes as the old and young were separated, and the shock of the experience, has stayed with me to this day. I was taken to Częstochowa, about 50 kilometres east of Kielce. From there I was transported to Dachau, which is a few kilometres north of Munich. Whilst on the train to Germany, valuable possessions were taken from me and the other people by a guard who told us that he would be taking the items to a bank for safe keeping. The train moved off but he never returned. When we arrived at Dachau we were assigned to forced work duties.

Although the food at Dachau was mediocre, I did not starve. On one occasion a lavish meal was laid on with good quality meat, vegetables and cake. I subsequently discovered that the meal had been laid on because of a Red Cross visit from Switzerland. The next day, of course, the food again became very basic. In an attempt to 'Germanise' us we were taught the German language, some of which I still remember.

From Dachau I was taken to Bavaria where the German language

• Fig. 13:16

125

dialect was different and hence more difficult to understand. There, together with 3 other Polish girls, I was required to work in a boys' boarding school, on cleaning, laundry and kitchen duties. The boys, aged 8 to 14, were the sons of high ranking Nazi officers. I worked there until American troops liberated the town and the boarding school. Amongst them were American Poles who wanted to take reprisals against any German who had mistreated us. Still frightened, I reported that I had not been treated cruelly but that the work had been very hard. The Red Cross and Poles from America played a major part in looking after the girls who worked at the boarding school.

I wanted to return to my parents in Poland, and made two attempts to go back. On each occasion, however, as no connecting trains had been laid on in Poland, we returned to Germany. When a third train was made available for those who wished to travel to Poland I told my friends that I would remain behind to look after our digs as they would only be back within a couple of days. As luck would have it, the third train made it to Poland. There was never to be a fourth train.

My next decision was to continue my education. I had heard that there were Polish schools in Italy being run by teachers attached to the Polish II Corps. With all my possessions in a small suitcase, I was attached to a group that was taken to the Italian border. On arrival we were interrogated by a Polish Captain to determine whether any of us were Germans attempting to escape to safety. I was asked, then strongly encouraged, to join the Polish Army where I would earn a little money, be looked after and have a more comfortable lifestyle. After filling in various forms I was accepted and allocated to Ancona as a member of the personal support staff to General Anders.

When the time came for the II Corps to be transferred to Britain and enlist into the PRC, I was assigned to an army family and resettled in England. It seems to me that the transferral was an administrative procedure as it took no account of people's expectations or desires. After we arrived at Liverpool I was soon transferred to Chandler's Ford, near Southampton. There I met my future husband Stanisław Lis, a sergeant in the Polish Army. We married and in 1947 moved to Tweedsmuir Camp. We moved to South West London in 1951.

Maria and Edward Modzelan's story:

Maria and Edward (Fig. 13:17) met in Italy after the war, and were married in Saint Biagio Church in Ravanna in north-eastern Italy. They lived in Tweedsmuir Camp until 1957.

Maria Modzelan (maiden name Jurowicz) was born on 5th January 1922. When war broke out she was placed in German captivity and was forced to work in German occupied Austria. Maria's German work permit (Fig. 13:18) shows that her captors made efforts to 'Germanise' her surname by spelling it "Jurowitsch", which she changed back to Polish immediately after arriving in Britain.

• Fig. 13:17

At the end of the war she was met by Polish officers from the Polish II Corps, who were scouring German displacement camps for Polish citizens. She was transferred to Italy, where the Corps was stationed, and placed under the protection of the Polish Army. There she met and married Edward, a Polish soldier serving with the Second Corps. The first 3 waves of Polish Army units, including the unit in which Edward had served, were transferred from Italy to Britain during the fourth quarter of 1946. Although married, Maria and Edward travelled to the United Kingdom separately. She arrived in Britain in October 1946 and was accommodated at Hiltingbury Transit Camp, Chandlers Ford. Edward arrived in November 1946 and was quartered at Jasper Camp, which was part of the Witley group of military camps in Surrey. On the 19 August 1947 Maria was transferred to Tweedsmuir Camp where Edward joined her after being demobilised. While Maria was refused permission to seek employment in Britain, Edward seems to have had three jobs while

• Fig. 13:18

127

living at Tweedsmuir.

They had one son, Józef, who was born at Diddington Hospital, St Neots, Huntingdonshire (now in Cambridgeshire). He was baptised in Tweedsmuir Camp chapel. His godparents were Wacław Pawiełko and Janina Wielkowska.

In 2001 Maria Modzelan received compensation from the Austrian authorities for her time in forced labour.

Wiesław Rogalski's ' story:

Wies (Fig. 13:19) was six years old when he left Tweedsmuir Camp with his family and therefore his education was completed in London.

Having qualified as a teacher of Biology, I taught at schools and a Further Education college in South London. My career included running field trips to Wales to study the ecology of the Pembrokeshire coast, the training of newly qualified teachers for the Inner London Education Authority, and working for the Qualification Curriculum Authority on education standards in vocational training programmes. I then became involved in the design and delivery of training programmes for the caring professions. For the last ten years of my career I worked with dyslexic students, having qualified as a Dyslexic Specialist. I worked with students on various vocational courses helping them access their programmes of study.

• Fig. 13:19

My adolescence was spent in Battersea, South London, where my parents had bought a house. It was an enjoyable time, as I tried to make the most of the opportunities London could offer. I remember going on trips to Central London; to museums and galleries and to see the Christmas lights on Regents Street. When we arrived in London we did not possess a television and so a weekly visit to the cinema was a must. There were four cinemas near our house, the Granada, the Empire, the Century and the

Esoldo. It was in these cinemas that I saw the Carry On films, Norman Wisdom, Kenneth Moore, The King and I, Cliff Richard and so on. I had two sets of friends, those from the English community and those from the Polish community, which of course was a luxury. I attended the Clapham Saturday morning Polish school run by the local parish where I was introduced to Polish history and geography. I must admit that I resented getting up early on Saturdays, something my English friends did not have to do. As my friends went to 'Saturday morning pictures' I had to sit in a stuffy classroom studying. As an older student I worked part-time in an electrical factory, which I did not enjoy. I am sure that mum and dad wanted me to experience tough manual labour in order to get me to work harder at school. I learnt much about life from working, while a student, at Peter Jones and Harvey Nichols department stores. These were central London stores and the clientele was usually very rich. Meeting all types of people there widened my horizons and aspirations.

• Fig. 13:20

I married in 1975 and moved to the Epsom area where we bought a house. This entailed me leaving South London where my parents lived but being not too far away I was able to visit them frequently. At the time of writing our son, who became a mechanical engineer, is working in Australia. My wife is also of Polish extraction and has an extensive family in Poland, whom we visit regularly. We are now enjoying retirement after 37 years of work.

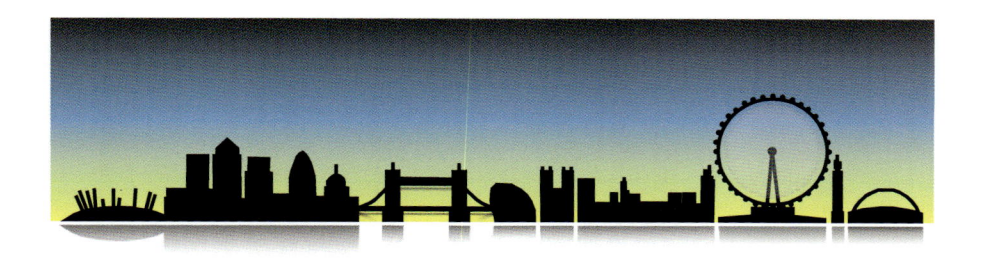

Zenon Rogalski's story:

Zen (Fig. 13:21) was 9 years old when his mother, father and brother moved out of Tweedsmuir in August 1957 to settle in SW London. His story, like that of his brother's, reflects the opportunities London had to offer.

My working life started in 1965 as a trainee structural engineer with Clarke, Nichols and Marcel, which was established in 1947 in Hammersmith, London. This was soon followed by a change in direction as engineering somehow didn't seem to match my expectations.

• Fig. 13:21

In 1966 I started training as a teacher and, although there were moments when the job became overwhelming, I never looked back until 2007 when I took early retirement due to personal commitments. Despite having completed my training as a teacher of physics and biology, my restlessness got the better of me again so in 1976 I decided that my chosen subjects were too turgid and tedious. Hence I retrained as a teacher of design, which gave me greater enjoyment, greater scope to be myself and the satisfaction of enabling pupils to learn through their senses by developing their different styles of learning. I knew this was the right move because very soon after I was running my own department in a school in Sevenoaks, Kent and within the space of six years was appointed one of Kent's Design Co-ordinators with a responsibility for co-ordinating the subject across 5 secondary schools, including the one at which I was the Head of Department (HoD).

As co-ordinator it became apparent to me that there was a need for Year 10 pupils in primary schools to have a better understanding of secondary school education thus making their transition from 'small school' to 'big school' easier. So, with the support from various quarters, I invited 10 to 11 year old children from local primary schools, their teachers and their parents to take part in an annual Design Day organised and manned by staff from my department. This may have been the event that prompted my County Advisor to invite me, as one of five HoDs from Kent, to participate in a new national Middle Management course that was certificated by Cambridge University.

In 1987 I was invited by Professor Richard Kimbell to serve on the Assessment of Performance Unit (APU) at Goldsmiths College, University of London. The APU was the major research arm of the Department for Education and Science. Its purpose was "to survey school populations to identify national capability levels"; in this case, in Design and Technology.

Soon after I was honoured to have been elected as one of two Teacher Governors for the school I was working at, a role that I continued to fulfil until I changed jobs in 1990.

At about this time the National Curriculum became a major cornerstone in the governments' education policy. I became acutely aware that my achievements placed me in a position from which I could help teachers deliver the 'new' curriculum. Having applied for advisory posts I was appointed Advisory Teacher Design with the London Borough of Bexley. My remit was to collaborate with others at the education authority in the delivery of design education to secondary schools. Due to internal changes my role soon expanded to include design education in primary schools and special needs education.

In 1993 I joined the staff of Alleyn's, a prestigious independent school in London, as Head of Design. This was an experience that has left me with many fond memories of working with highly motivated professionals and pupils. I feel a deep satisfaction that many of my pupils became designers, one of whom proudly announced in 1998 that a private exhibition of his work was at a London gallery. While many of

• **Fig. 13:22** Zen Rogalski being introduced to Lord Carey of Clifton (Archbishop of Canterbury 1991 - 2002) by Dr Colin Niven (Headmaster Alleyn's School 1992 - 2002) in 1998

my students chose a career in architecture, others became product designers, and interior designers.

At the time of writing I share my life with my wife of 40 years, enjoying the company of our daughter who works as a Senior Rights Negotiator in the music industry, son-in-law and two granddaughters.

The Rogalskis as singer/songwriters:

At the ages of 17 (Wies) and 19 (Zen), we started to compose songs and perform at various South London clubs (Fig. 13:23). Our song writing gave us the chance to meet some of the most influential figures in the music industry and other celebrities of the time. For example, Mickie Most and his brother Dave Most, who owned *RAK* records were two individuals with whom we met. They recorded and produced artists such as Sweet, Mud, and Suzi Quatro. We also met song writers Nicky Chinn and Mike Chapman, albeit briefly.

Larry Page was another interesting person with whom we discussed 'things musical'. He was the producer/manager of acts such as The Kinks and The Troggs, recording them on his own *Page One* records, and subsequently *Penny Farthing* records. Larry Page is also credited with producing *Blue is the Colour* for 'Chelsea Football Club': a team we started to support soon after we came to London.

• **Fig. 13:23** Wies (left) and Zen (right) Rogalski performing in 1968

When we were in our late 20s we met Richard Sims, a promising record producer who recorded many of our songs. In those days recordings were done on a reel to reel analogue machine: much more fun than sitting in front of a computer screen.

By this time, of course, both of us were working as teachers, but the weekends and holidays became our private time when we promoted our joint musical activities. Producing a song in a professional, 24 track studio is one thing but promoting awareness of the song to the public is another. A much larger organisation is an advantage for such an undertaking. To this end we endeavoured to attract the attention of some of the most influential musicians and promoters of that era. David Paramor, who worked as Artist and Repertoire Manager (or A&R Man) at *Dick James Music* was someone who was interested in our work. David Paramor was the son of Norrie Paramor, a gifted and successful musician who, among other achievements, was orchestral conductor at the London Palladium, Recording Director at EMI's *Columbia* records, and producer of artists such as Helen Shapiro, Cliff Richard (now Sir Cliff Richard), and The Shadows.

Dick James was a successful musical promoter in his own right. He owned *Dick James Music*, and its subsidiaries *Dick James Publishing* and *DJM* records. In collaboration with Brian Epstein, he also established *Northern Songs*, a publishing house for The Beatles' first compositions.

David Paramor was particularly keen on two of our songs, "You Can Never Win (my love from me)" and "Come Back For More." However, before he could commit himself, he informed us that he had to have them approved by Dick James. We left the material with him and awaited a response. In the meantime we kept an appointment we had made previously with *Chelsea* records who were equally impressed with the same songs, promising to release them as a single and talk about future recordings. Euphoria clouded our thinking as we took the decision to go back to David Paramor a few days later, asking for the return of our compositions. His graciousness at this request continues to live vividly in our minds. A few days after that, *Chelsea* records retracted their interest and we were left with compositions that promised so much but delivered very little.

Every song has its moment, and although we tried to capture other record companies' attention with our songs, the moment had passed. It was a dreadful error of judgement.

Although stardom was not to come, even though it was nice to dream, we did manage to have five songs published and they remain on the *Performing Rights Society* (PRS) database to this day.

Individual achievements in brief:

In this part of the chapter we have collated a short list of Polish people who lived as children in Tweedsmuir Camp together with their achievements in adulthood. The intention is not to create an exhaustive record but to indicate how some of the descendants of the first generation 'Tweedsmuirians' have fared.

Danuta Czertko: Worked in Barclays Bank before going into the catering profession. A few years after that became an interior designer before having a family.

Włodzimiesz Diemko: Qualified as a chemist. Conducted scientific translations. Became councillor for Hounslow; encouraged the development of Saturday morning Polish school in Chiswick. He is married to Stasia Horwat, a Polish opera singer.

Janusz Gąsiorowski: Qualified as a dentist. His surgery was in Shepherd's Bush, London. He and his family now live in Ealing, London.

Wacek Gąsiorowski: Brother of Janusz. Structural Engineer. Spent 25 years working abroad. Worked in Kenya designing bridges, one of which is named after him. He became chief engineer for Rhodes Engineering Group Ltd. Wacek's wife went to the prestigious St Martin's School of Art.

Janusz and Wacek's father was one of the Polish Officers killed at Katyn. Their mother married Jan Raubo after the war. He became the first President of the Polish ex-Combatants Association at Tweedsmuir Camp. They had a girl called Hania and lived at number 38 Tweedsmuir Camp. At the age of 17, Hania worked as a dental nurse at Janusz's dental practice.

Danusia Goryniewska: Finished a languages degree. Taught English language in Yemen.

• **Fig. 13:24** Hania Raubo on the right. In the middle is Zen Rogalski and next to him Wies Rogalski

Krystyna Goryniewska: Sister of Danusia. Attended St Martin's School of Art. Went to America. Worked at the United Nations (UN). Became a UN Representative in one of the Middle East countries (country unknown).

Alicia Walak (maiden name Michalska): Became a secretary for a solicitor's firm whose clients included artists from the popular music industry. Her son, Robert Walak (Fig. 13:25), is a third generation 'Tweedsmuirian' and a film producer. His filmography includes *Lesbian Vampire Killers*, directed by Phil Claydon (2009); *The King's Speech*, directed by Tim Hooper (2010); *Shame*, directed by Steve McQueen (2011); *Weekender*, directed by Carl Golden (2011), and *U Want Me 2 Kill Him?*, directed by Andrew Douglas (in development at the time of writing).

Fig. 13:25 Robert Walak, film producer

Krystyna Karas (maiden name Obara): Daughter of Maria Obara. Krystyna qualified as an optician. She married a petroleum engineer, and lives with her family in the house her parents bought in South West London after they moved away from Tweedsmuir Camp. Previously the Karas family lived in Sevenoaks, Kent.

Eva Kot: Worked as a translator in Spain and Mexico City. When she returned to the UK, Eva secured a position as a translator in the City, which gave her the opportunity to work as an insurance broker for a syndicate at Lloyds. Following this, Eva started a family.

Zbigniew Lis: Qualified as an accountant, specialising in turning around failing businesses. He has gained a reputation for accomplishing what others argue cannot be done. His goal has always been to save people's jobs, which he has achieved many times over.

Chapter 14

Final Comments

Remains of the Motor Transport Garage next to the Thursley Road entrance

Today, the camp system, of which Tweedsmuir was part, is a distant memory. In earlier chapters we have tried to explain why the system existed and how it functioned by focussing on the history of Tweedsmuir Camp and the people who were accommodated there. The object of this chapter is to draw thought provoking conclusions from the central elements mentioned in the previous chapters. Each of the elements is analysed under subheadings.

Issues in writing the final comments

We were mindful of two issues while writing the final comments about the community of Polish people who lived in Tweedsmuir Camp immediately after World War Two. The first issue centres on the fact that Tweedsmuir was used to accommodate the 501 Basic Unit, PRC who were employed by the WO in the demobilisation of the Polish Forces at Witley Camp. This made Tweedsmuir unique as no other camp in the United Kingdom was designated that role. But as the PRC was being run down, civilians, the administrators' families and dependants, were transferred from safe havens to Tweedsmuir. This created a problem as to who was responsible for the inhabitants of Tweedsmuir Camp, causing a war of words between the WO and the NAB. The WO could not be responsible for civilians as this was the job of the NAB but, there was no mechanism in place for transferring the administration of a WO camp to the NAB. This problem was not resolved until the mid 1950s when Hambledon District Council took over the management of Tweedsmuir Camp.

The second issue was of a more personal nature. The history described both in the exhibition at the RLC, Tilford and in this booklet is laden with emotion, claim and counterclaim, anger, heroic martyrology and a people's determination to live a principled life. In short, it is a history that has been told by the post-war émigrés and hence one in which we have been completely immersed. Therefore this task was complicated by the fact that, having been members of this community, it was difficult to detach ourselves completely from the events discussed herein. Yet true dispassion should exist in the writing of history.

The United Nations Declaration

The existence of the post-WWII Polish population in Britain was a sign that there were unforeseen problems for the Allies in the closing months of the war. There was no plan in the early stages of the war, or at war's end in 1945, for Britain to provide a refuge for people who feared returning to their own country: in this case a group of people who were reluctant to return to a communist led Poland, finding instead a modicum of peace in a quiet corner of Surrey.

On one level, placing about 70 families into Tweedsmuir was a success because it provided shelter and opportunity for a group of young families who had lost everything during the war: their homes, in some cases their relatives, and certainly the resources on which to live. Tweedsmuir offered the chance to begin again and this has to be acknowledged and celebrated. However, the existence of a Polish population in Thursley was also a sign of failure, which stretched back to 1 January 1942 when on that day, President Roosevelt, Prime Minister Churchill, Maxim Litvinov, Soviet Ambassador to the United States of America, and TV Soong, Premier of the

Republic of China, signed a short document which later came to be known as the *United Nations Declaration*. The following day representatives of 22 other nations, among them Poland, also signed. This declaration was effected in the light of the Atlantic Charter, the third principle of which was to "… respect the right of all peoples to choose the form of government under which they will live; and … to see sovereign rights and self government restored to those who have been forcibly deprived of them." Yet this noble statement of principle was disregarded under the Teheran and Yalta agreements eventually leading to the formation of the PGNU. The PGNU was recognised by France and Sweden on 29 June 1945. The United States and Great Britain subsequently recognised it on 5 July. Later, the governments of nearly all other states followed suit. The Vatican, along with Spain and Ireland, for example, did not recognised the PGNU until 1979. Arguably, for the Polish in the West, this sequence of events represented an inconstancy in ***international*** diplomacy.

A compromise and an astonishing plan

It seems to us that the formation of the PRC was the result of a compromise made in 1946 between British and Polish authorities in the West. This compromise allowed Polish Forces, and Polish refugees, who did not return to Poland, to settle in Britain thus removing the threats that were being made by the Polish high command to initiate military action against the Red Army in Poland. To explain how and why this scenario came about, brings into play an element of Second World War history that has only recently come to light.

In April 1945 the Western Allies had met with the Red Army in central Europe. Sir Winston Churchill was so concerned about the Soviet's behaviour after Yalta that he astonished his chiefs of staff by enquiring whether a force comprising, American, British, German and Polish troops could launch an offensive to drive the Soviets out of East Germany back to the USSR. For planning purposes the proposed campaign was codenamed Operation *Unthinkable* and the target date for its launch was to have been 1 July 1945. In Churchill's words, the aim of *Unthinkable* was to get "a square deal for Poland" by removing Soviet troops from Eastern Europe. The highly secretive and sensitive nature of the operation prompted

General Hastings Ismay to write in a memorandum to Churchill that the chiefs of staff thought that "... the less we put on paper on this subject the better." Only a very tight circle of military planners knew of its existence, including General Dwight Eisenhower. As Polish Forces formed part of the proposal for Operation *Unthinkable* there is every likelihood that the Polish Commander-in-Chief, General Anders, and some of his most trusted Polish military aides, were also privy to the details. If this was the case, just how serious was the proposal considered to be?

Irrespective of how this issue is addressed it is extremely likely that for the Polish Forces the aim of Operation *Unthinkable* was precisely the kind of offensive that was required to deal with the USSR's annexation of eastern Poland, or *Kresy*. With special permission from Field Marshal Alexander, General Anders continued to screen and recruit Polish soldiers, including those who were previously conscripted into the *Wehrmacht*. By 8 May 1945 the strength of the Polish II Corps rose to 75,581: an increase of 60% from April the previous year and a number that does not include auxiliary staff. In *The Formation of the Polish Community in Great Britain 1939-50*, Norman Davis explains that from this increase in personnel "several new formations were created." The creation of new Polish Army units, however, poses the question as to why the British and Polish military leaders would seek to increase the strength of the Polish Army in Italy when,

- the war was coming to an end,

- the Nazi leadership was preparing to surrender unconditionally, which it did on 7 May, and

- preparations were being made to celebrate Victory in Europe on 8 May?

We consider it feasible to suggest that, given the information available, the answer centres on the probability that the senior Polish military leaders may have been preparing to take part in Operation *Unthinkable*. However, when the final report was delivered on 22 May 1945, the conclusion was that "the result of a total war with Russia is not possible to forecast, but the one thing certain is that to win it would take us a very long time." Later Sir Alan Brooke wrote in his diary, "the idea is, of course, fantastic and the chances of success quite impossible." Operation *Unthinkable* was shelved. In line with what was happening in Central Europe at the time, the main anxiety now was for Polish individuals to return home from various parts of the European continent and the Middle East and to take part in the imminent Polish elections.

The morale of Polish high command was strained further, however, when the Polish Government in Warsaw issued a statement on 14 February 1946 that it no longer recognised the land, sea and air formations in the West as units of the Polish Forces. At this point every man and woman in the Polish Forces became stateless, and without citizenship. They were armed and disgruntled. Relations between the Warsaw Government, the British Government and the Polish Forces were now so impossible that Attlee and Bevin changed tack. In May 1946 Bevin announced that he was now aiming to demobilise the Polish II Corps. The demobilisation of the Polish Airforce and Polish Navy would soon follow.

Historians seem to agree that the transformation of the illustrious Polish II Corps into a resettlement corps was probably one of the last events in the long saga of Anglo-Polish friction during World War Two. Political opinion in Britain seemed to accept, albeit without much enthusiasm, that this was the best solution to a very difficult problem. The first enrolment into the PRC took place on 13 September 1946.

The PRC process and demobilisation

The history of the PRC has often been misrepresented by the use of words to describe its function. For example, giving Polish ex-soldiers the chance to **integrate**, or to **assimilate** into life in Britain, or to become "**fully adjusted** to British life." Since this was not the purpose of the Corps, just how accurate are such claims?

When Earnest Bevin announced in the House of Commons the formation of the PRC he described it as an administrative "transitional arrangement, designed to facilitate the transition (of PRC personnel) from military to civil life, whether in British territory **or in foreign countries**." The brochure, *Polish*

Resettlement Corps - Conditions of Service, published by the WO in August 1946 carried the same statement. For the British Government, then, the PRC prepared Polish servicemen for civilian life either in Britain or overseas. Moreover, from the outset, even when in the PRC its personnel were repeatedly encouraged to repatriate or to emigrate to another country.

The PRC process was fraught with errors underpinned by, according to Keith Sword, an "ad hoc administrative machinery that had sprung up to cope with the many facets of demobilisation and resettlement of Polish servicemen and women in civilian life." Yet it was also a success. 105,053 Polish servicemen and women started a new life abroad of which over 91,000 settled in Britain. In time the number of Polish people who stayed in post-war Britain increased as service personnel were reunited with families and dependants. Enlisting in the resettlement corps enabled them to start thinking about their future; to purchase houses, furniture, clothes, and technological innovations such as televisions, washing machines, and refrigerators. The PRC mechanism also aided the Polish individuals in settling among their British neighbours. Despite the effectiveness of the PRC, senior British and Polish officials recognised that it had a limited lifespan.

When the PRC was finally wound up in 1949, "there was a widespread feeling that the problem had been brought to a satisfactory resolution", states Ciechanowski. There was much self-congratulatory backslapping among the British and Polish high command. Both parties agreed that the resettlement of Polish ex-soldiers, their families and dependants had "been solved beyond the extent of early expectations." Civilian leaders too announced their satisfaction that the PRC process had been completed successfully. In October in the House of Commons, for example, the Secretary of State for War (Emanuel Shinwell) confirmed that "ex-members of the PRC are living either in private accommodation or in the hostels of the NAB." However, the fact that the vast majority of these hostels were 'converted' military barracks seems to have been omitted from the euphoric rhetoric.

In 1951 the MoL and NS completed a "final analysis" of PRC statistics, which were published on 14 February as a table that is reproduced below (Fig. 14:1). For the sake of expediency, by late 1948 to early 1949 the small number of Polish ex-sailors were incorporated into the Army figures.

Summary	Army	RAF	Total
Repatriated	8,542	442	8,984
Emigrated	10,861	1,414	12,275
Wastage (Deceased personnel)	1,338	40	1,378
Relinquished Commission Cases	1,928	542	2,470
Resettled in Employment etc	67,607	5,355	72,962
Enlisted into Services (Army)	405	504	909
Students	1,599	467	2,066
Discharge from Effective Strength	10,867	2,126	12,993
Total	103,147	10,890	114,037

• Fig. 14:1

Forming a community and resettlement

When the 501 Basic Unit, PRC under the command of Colonel Berendt first entered Tweedsmuir Camp in July 1947 it was a random group of soldiers. In due course they were reunited with their civilian relatives who had been transferred from the so called safe havens.

As the PRC was being run down, all the Polish ex- service personnel became answerable to British civilian law as laid down by the *Polish Resettlement Act,* 1947. It is at this point that the history of Tweedsmuir Camp and its inhabitants becomes chaotic because there was no provision for transferring the administration of a WO camp, housing Polish WO employees, to the NAB. The situation rumbled on until 1949. Although the WO had threatened to close the camp by 31 December, its officials allowed the Polish residents to remain in the camp due to pressure from the Polish Ex-Combatants Association. This was probably the defining moment in the formation of the Tweedsmuir Camp community. (It may be of interest to note that the Resettlement Act remained on the statute book until 2008 when it was removed by the Lord Chancellor and Justice Secretary Jack Straw.)

The main stimuli that influenced the formation of the community was shared by all of the Polish II Corps soldiers:

- deportation from their homeland to work camps deep inside the USSR (although a few 'Tweedsmuirians' had been deported to work camps in Nazi Germany),
- a common experience of war,
- religious beliefs and practises,
- cultural background,
- the Polish language,
- losing families and belongings,
- making new families, and the reunification of family groups created in Poland.

All of these stimuli, except the first, were also relevant for the Polish airmen and sailors who had enrolled in the PRC.

The camp was situated in an area in which the Polish community felt free to express their customs and culture by organising Corpus Christi processions, First Holy Communion ceremonies and the Polish-Lithuanian 3 May Constitution celebrations. In this respect it was their territory. Politics, language, and religion, for example, were indisputably strong influences that resulted in individuals relating to each other. Such influences were without doubt the common denominators that determined the character of the Tweedsmuir community. The losses and war-time experiences of the first Tweedsmuir generation helped them to form strong social bonds. They looked to each other for assistance as their English language skills were weak and because their knowledge of the British way of life was limited. In other words, they formed an *introspective* community (our definition).

Once the Tweedsmuir community dispersed, territory was less of an influence on their outlook than were the elements of, for example, the Polish language, religion and ethnic origin, which had provided them with a common identity. Moreover, whether in Guildford, Milford or South West London, individuals had to change and adapt to a more British way of life despite their common Polish characteristics. Moving out of the camp gave families a greater opportunity to integrate into British society.

Integrating into British society

As an introspective community the chances of integrating into British society were limited for the first 'Tweedsmuirians' because, on the whole, they tended not to form relationships or to interact with individuals living in villages surrounding the camp.

Few would argue with the precept that the greater contact an individual has with different kinds of people, the less likely it becomes for that individual to be treated as an outsider. Additionally, choosing to voluntarily segregate oneself from others by withdrawing into one's own community, presents fewer opportunities to engage with characteristics of human nature. Thus, after the camp closed, moving into areas that were predominantly non-Polish provided Tweedsmuir individuals with greater opportunities to become part of a multicultural society.

Legislation can smooth the way for individuals to integrate. For example, the Attlee government helped Polish ex-soldiers settle in Britain by passing the *Polish Resettlement Act* in 1947. Among other things, the Act eased the Polish individuals' progress into work and provided them with access to education and affordable housing. Programmes to learn English had also been established as had "instruction about English ways in general." However, the ***act of integrating*** is a personal choice, which cannot be legislated for. It is a desire that comes from within, particularly where, for instance, friendships, relationships, acts of worship, and the like are involved. Equally, psychological issues such as the way people think, how they view themselves and their surroundings cannot be legislated for either. With this in mind, the integration of Tweedsmuir individuals would always be in doubt unless they were prepared to engage in such initiatives, and were able to overcome the psychological trauma they had experienced during the war. This may have led to closure, as it is called today, before readjusting to a new way of life whether in Britain or another country.

Although we would argue that the first generation 'Tweedsmuirians' found it difficult to integrate, their children have been better able to 'slip in and out' of the British way of life. Arguably, while the third generation 'Tweedsmuirians' have integrated with the greatest of ease, the fourth generation, which is in its infancy at the time of writing, will more than likely read this history concerning their great grandparents in their school textbooks.

Hoping to return to Poland after the Korean War

For the vast majority of the post-war Polish individuals in Britain, the PRC process was a temporary measure as they anticipated a return to Poland under more favourable political conditions. This state of mind remained with them until 1953 when the Korean war ended. They perceived the issue of Korea as the last defining moment of WWII. During their summit meetings, the Allies discussed the future of the Japanese Empire. In the short term, pending the return of Korean independence, Korea, a Japanese colony since 1910, was to be influenced north of the 38th parallel by Soviet Russia. To the south, a United States military administration under the direction of General D MacArthur would control the area from its headquarters in Tokyo.

Following a number of frontier confrontations, the Republic of Korea was invaded on 25 June 1950 by the North Korean Peoples' Army. As the war unfolded, it developed into a conflict between forces from 21 UN countries and 2 communist countries: the Soviet Union and the Peoples' Republic of China. The ex-PRC individuals argued that once the UN forces had defeated the communists, a new order would be established in eastern Europe, permitting them to return to Poland. When this did not occur, the post-war Polish émigrés in Britain, as well as around the world, resigned themselves to remaining outside Poland's borders.

A question of European refugees

Between 1943 and 1944, during the Italian campaign, the Allies found themselves attending to the needs of millions of civilian refugees. A similar scenario unfolded in Germany following the D-Day campaign. It soon became apparent that foot soldiers were ill-equipped to deal with this problem. To this end, the governments of America, Britain and the Soviet Union acted by forming the United Nations Relief and Rehabilitation Administration (UNRRA). Its role was to bring humanitarian aid to civilian refugees by providing shelter in disused concentration camps, food, medical care, and a rapid repatriation programme.

At the same time émigrés, intellectuals, and relief workers were attempting to influence those responsible for managing the UNRRA. The leading voices in this debate were on the political left; internationalists opposed to war. Their work produced a construct, as Ben Shepherd calls it, that would define, in the process, an agreed model of the post-war landscape, and, in particular, the future of a concept: the Displaced Person. It is unclear where the phrase originated, but it was not in use in 1939. By 1943, however, the idea of the 'Displaced Person' had entered into the international vocabulary and, argues Professor G. Cohen, was used during WWII to help detect, "true" and "false" refugees in occupied *Germany and Austria*. This posed a serious problem for the British Government who were responsible for Polish Forces around the world; an issue that will be addressed in due course.

When the dust of war had settled, there remained about one million people in countries such as Austria, Germany, Italy and Switzerland, who were disinclined to return to their place of origin. What is more, the latter stages of WWII also saw the forced migration of German citizens from Poland and Czechoslovakia, mostly into areas which would become post-war Germany and post-war Austria. Serious disagreements erupted when arguments were put forward by the Soviet and American decision-makers that all German citizens were ineligible to receive UNRRA aid. This gave rise to an important principle being established. Only UN civilian nationals, stateless persons, UN Prisoners of War, and some categories of internally displaced Italian citizens were eligible to receive UNRRA help. These individuals were grouped together as "Displaced Persons", which was a term reserved "for a certain class" of refugee, entitling them to "special care and support." Enemy nationals, ethnic German civilians, and collaborators of the enemy, were not included in this group and were not provided with aid by UNRRA. Prior to this, in 1943, Churchill had outlined a plan to provide "food and freedom" to the

German civilian refugees but this was quietly discarded as it became clear that the plan would be opposed by the smaller nations of Western Europe who were already angry that they had been excluded from UNRRA's administrative circles.

The humanitarian needs of the German refugees were taken up by, for example, the *Deutscher Caritasverband (DCV)* (the German Caritas Movement), which was one of seven welfare organisations left largely intact after the war. Shephard contends that as a consequence of these developments the phrase 'displaced person' became "shorthand for Hitler's victims" as it defined a "mental construct for the rest of the decade."

Once the UNRRA principles were used to manage refugees, the British Government faced a serious issue regarding the Polish Forces under its command who were refusing to repatriate. The Polish Forces were obviously not civilians or Prisoners of War, nor were the vast majority of them held captive in Germany or Austria at the time. The Polish Army personnel who were accommodated at Tweedsmuir Camp after the war were previously stationed in Ancona, Italy. There they were 'fed and watered', accommodated, clothed, and received a British soldiers pay from the WO in London. They did not require any humanitarian assistance, as refugees or displaced persons, from UNRRA and so were given three options: to repatriate, or to emigrate to another country, or to enlist in the PRC. Those who chose to enlist in the PRC did so as soldiers whose rights were covered by the Geneva Convention. Those who decided to repatriate either remained in the Polish Forces or were demobilised in Poland. The remainder were demobilised on entry into the country of their choice (eg Australia) and then were treated as refugees, receiving the same aid under the UNRRA scheme as civilian 'displaced persons' in Europe. At the behest of the British Government, administration of the dependants and families of PRC personnel in safe havens was in the hands of UNRRA up to 1947 and, post-1947, the International Refugee Organisation (IRO). By the time the PRC had been wound up in September 1949, Louise Holborn, the IRO historian was claiming that "the Organisation had under its mandate only refugees." Hence the civilians in Tweedsmuir were closer to being refugees or, possibly, 'political refugees'. Their welfare was taken care of under the provisions written in the *Polish Resettlement Act* of 1947. Besides, it was the end of a decade they would probably have preferred to forget; it did not really matter what label they were given. Like other people around the world, the 'Tweedsmuirians' had to look forward, as had leaders of nation-states who sought ways of undoing the damage of war. In 1967 the Geneva Convention on the status of refugees stipulated that refugees in their host countries "must at least enjoy the rights of non-refugee foreigners."

Before leaving this subject, it is worthwhile noting that the displaced person status was fiercely contested at the end of the war as many refugees tried to obtain the generous benefits on offer. This problem became so acute that the terms refugees and displaced persons became the principle concerns of international debate, which has lead to the following three internationally recognised definitions:

Refugee - First, anyone who has been considered a refugee under the Arrangements of 12 May 1926 and 30 June 1928 or under the Conventions of 28 October 1933 and 10 February 1938, the Protocol of 14 September 1939, the Constitution of the International Refugee Organisation, or the 1951 Convention.

Second, a person who is outside their own country and is unable or unwilling to return due to a well-founded fear of being persecuted because of their, race religion, nationality, membership of a particular social group, or political opinion.

Internally Displaced Persons - Persons or groups of persons who have been forced or obliged to flee or to leave their homes or places of habitual residence, in particular as a result of or in order to avoid the effects of armed conflict, situations of generalised violence, violations of human rights or natural or human-made disasters, and who have not crossed an internationally recognised State border.

Asylum Seeker: An asylum seeker is a person who has fled their own country and applied for protection as a refugee.

The 'Displaced Person' was no longer in existence as a term. When the IRO took over responsibility for WWII refugees in 1946 the Organisation's hierarchy became astounded at the harm caused by segregating refugees deserving of aid, and those who were not. So appalled were the IRO executives that up to the end of 1947 the overwhelming majority of DPs, as identified by UNRRA, were "treated as permanent asylum seekers." Post-1947, as we have seen, all people deserving humanitarian aid were called refugees.

Kultura and an Alternative Point of View

At the same time as UNRRA was wrestling with the difficult task of identifying refugees eligible for humanitarian aid, a small group of Polish intellectuals had established a publication called *Kultura* (Fig. 14:2) which, according to Professor Timothy Snyder of Yale University, was one of the principle influences on the birth of a new Polish nation-state in 1989.

Kultura was first published in 1946 in Paris as a monthly journal. Its editor was Jerzy Giedroyć who had served under General Anders in Italy as Head of the Polish II Corps Publishing Department. Giedroyć and his inner-most circle of seven writers settled in Paris rather than London after the war as it was always assumed that the socio-political perspective of *Kulutra* was progressive, contrasting sharply with the backward looking Polish establishment in London.

• Fig. 14:2

Kultura editorials advised resolving differences between Poland and the nations on her eastern borders: Soviet Belarus, Soviet Lithuania and Soviet Ukraine; later Belarus, Lithuania and Ukraine. From France, the journal tried to influence Polish politics and political thinking. In this Giedroyć differed from other Polish émigrés in the West who sought to preserve the nature and political structure of interwar (1918-1939) Poland. While many Polish ex-diplomats in London saw no reason why they should accept the loss of eastern territories to Soviet Russia, Giedroyć saw the new Poland evolving along the lines of a modern nation-state: a concept that was alien to traditionalists at the time, claims Snyder. Professor Snyder also contends that Giedroyć believed that Belarus, Lithuania and Ukraine could also become nation-states as he recognised that the end of WWII did not settle Poland's eastern border. He endeavoured to produce a plan that would give a future Poland the opportunity to seek new solutions to address this issue. To the Polish Government in London this was dissension of the worst kind. Giedroyć's plan became known as the *Kultura* programme.

Supporters of *Kultura* accepted Poland's eastern frontier as the line agreed between Molotov and Ribbentrop in 1939, confirmed at the Yalta conference in 1945, and often referred to as the Curzon Line (Fig. 14:3). Giedroyć's unique plan was to treat Poland's *Kresy* not as territory lost to the Soviet Union but as contested land that could now be part of the newly emerging nation-states of Belarus, Lithuania and Ukraine.

Giedroyć had an associate by the name of Juliusz Mieroszewski who lived in London. Mieroszewski provided the intellectual rationale for the grand plan of a future Polish nation-state. In 1973 and 1974, he argued that at the centre of the plan was the future of a sovereign Poland, and that the agreements made at the end of the Second World War should not be reversed. He suggested that the Belarus, Lithuania and Ukraine nations be strengthened and that Poland should champion their independence. He contended that Poland should not seek to recover territories east of the Curzon Line, but support the aspirations of its Belarusian, Lithuanian and Ukrainian neighbours in seeking self-government.

According to Snyder, throughout the 1980s, Mieroszewski's arguments were considered in greater depth and at greater length. By 1989 the collective opinion in Poland was to establish good relations with their eastern neighbours. Snyder makes it very clear that the *Kultura* programme, a new progressive attitude in Poland to the previously accepted political point of view, underground publications, and Solidarność, not only opposed the recovery of eastern territories, but supported the independence of its neighbours in the east.

When the Polish communists failed to form a government in August 1989, a coalition government came into power under the leadership of Tadeusz Mazowiecki. Krzystof Skubiszewski was Poland's foreign minister from 12 September 1989 to 25 October 1993. He was very much in favour of Giedroyć's and Mieroszewski's basic political arguments, but preferred to use the phrase "state interest" instead of "national interest." Between October 1990 and December 1991, Foreign Minister Skubiszewski was instrumental in establishing agreements on borders between Poland and the newly unified Germany in the west, and Belarus, Lithuania, and Ukraine in the east. That December the Soviet Union ceased to exist. Skubiszewski was also at the centre of ensuring that Germany, Poland, Belarus, Lithuania and Ukraine would respect each others' territory, and, more importantly, each others' borders. He stressed and acknowledged that this was the way modern nation-states should behave in a modern Europe, leaving history to the historians, and politics to the politicians.

Five days after the death of Giedroyć in September 2000, Polish historian Adam Zamoyski described him in the Guardian as "a publisher who kept the spirit of a free Poland alive through the long years of communist rule."

◆   ◆   ◆

The children whose work is reproduced in the next chapter, were born just after the time the new Polish nation-state was formed. They have little knowledge of the history that is expressed in this publication except that which has been told to them by their parents (whose education was moulded by the USSR) and their grandparents. In conversation, the children stated that their families came to England for economic reasons which is in complete contrast to the reasons for the first 'Tweedsmuirians' coming to Britain.

In March 2011 we presented a brief illustrated history of Tweedsmuir Camp to the children at the Saturday morning Polish School in Milford, pointing out that the Poland the children at the school and indeed their teachers know, is not the Poland that the original inhabitants of Tweedsmuir Camp would have known.

These young people, as well as the grandchildren of the first generation 'Tweedsmuirians', represent the next phase of this history, which is untouched by the unfortunate circumstances of war. For their sake, long may this continue.

Chapter 15

Saturday morning Polish School at Milford, including children's work

Polska szkola sobotnia
im. Tadeusz Czuchnickiego

"Ave Maria", Milford, Portsmouth Road, GU8 5AU, United Kingdom

autorzy tekstu: Zofia Łuklińska i Marek Plaskota

Nasza Szkoła pod tym adresem działa nieprzerwanie od 1987 roku i jest kontynuacją szkoły sobotniej, która rozpoczęła swoją działalność w obozach demobilizacyjnych Wojska Polskiego na terenie hrabstwa Surrey w Wielkiej Brytanii.

Chociaż scena polityczna i pozycja Polski w świecie uległa kategorycznej zmianie od czasów drugiej wojny światowej, a potem w 1990 roku w okresie posolidarnościowym, cele szkoły pozostały prawie identyczne i równie patriotyczne.

Polska dołączyła do Unii Europejskiej w maju 2004 roku i od tego czasu Polacy mogą się swobodnie poruszać po Europie i bez żadnych trudności osiedlać się i podejmować pracę w krajach Unijnych. Sytuacja ta doprowadziła do znacznego zwiększenia się liczby Polaków mieszkających na terenie Wielkiej Brytanii.

Polacy zakładaja tutaj swoje nowe rodziny, tutaj przychodzą na świat ich dzieci, a w związku z tym istnieje potrzeba istnienia szkół polskich, które konsekwentnie nauczają dzieci i młodzież ojczystego jezyka, kultury, tradycji i miłości do Polski, ojczyzny ich rodziców. Dużą grupę uczniów szkoły w Milford stanowią dzieci urodzone w Polsce, których rodzice pragną by ich dzieci kontynuowały naukę języka ojczystego.

Nasza szkoła współpracuje ściśle z Polską Parafią w Milford i korzysta z pomieszczeń Domu Parafialnego, który wielkim staraniem został zakupiony i odremontowany przez polską społeczność na użytek tutejszych Polaków w czerwcu 1984 roku.
Proboszczem parafii był wówczas ksiądz Tadeusz Grzesik. Prezesem Parafii, i jednocześnie Prezesem Stowarzyszenia Polskich Kombatantów, Koła SPK Nr 107 na tych terenach był wtedy pan Tadeusz Czuchnicki.

Powojenna polska społeczność wywodziła się głównie z rodzin wojskowych stacjonujących na terenach hrabstwa Surrey, w tzw. obozach demobilizacyjnych utworzonych po zakończeniu II Wojny Światowej.

About the Saturday morning Polish School
In honour of our patron Tadeusz Czuchnicki

Authors: Zofia Łuklińska and Marek Plaskota

Our school has been based at its current address since 1987, although its origin is to be found in the post war Polish resettlement camps in Surrey.

Although Poland's political scene changed significantly after the Second World War and again after the emergence of Solidarity in 1990, the aims of the school have hardly changed and remain patriotic.

After Poland's entry into the European Union in May 2004, Polish citizens gained the freedom of movement to work and settle in other EU countries. This has led to a significant increase in the size of the Polish population in Great Britain.

On settling in Britain many began families, increasing the need for Polish schools. These schools continue to teach the language of their parents and foster a love of Poland: the homeland of their parents. Some families have come to Britain with children and their priority is to ensure that the children continue learning the Polish language.

Our school works closely with the Polish parish in Milford and makes use of its Parish Centre, which was bought and renovated in June 1984.

At that time the parish priest was Fr. Tadeusz Grzesik. The president of the parish, who was also the president of the 107 Polish Ex-Combatants Association, was Mr Tadeusz Czuchnicki.

The postwar Polish community originated mainly from military families of Forces stationed in Surrey, and who lived in the so called resettlement camps created after the Second War World.

After the closure of these camps, some families remained close to Godalming, Milford, Witley, Elstead, Thursley, and Guildford. Many moved to London or other parts of England seeking work and opportunities for their families.

Unfortunately, for many of them the road to Poland after the war was closed. Nevertheless, whilst cultivating a loyalty to their 'second homeland', they maintained their Polishness and their deep love for their motherland, its culture and traditions, and endeavoured to ensure that their children spoke the Polish language.

It is impossible to name every patriotic Polish individual but one,

Po likwidacji tych obozów wiele rodzin pozostało w okolicach Godalming, Milford, Witley, Elstead, Thursley, Plaistow, Guildford. Część osób wyjechała do Londynu lub innych miejscowości w Anglii w pogoni za pracą lub z przyczyn rodzinnych.

Niestety droga powrotna do Polski była dla większości z nich zamknięta. Wszyscy jednak pozostali lojalni swojej ojczyźnie, zachowali swoją polskość i głęboką miłość do Ojczyzny, która objawiała się uszanowaniem kultury i tradycji polskich, oraz przekazywaniem znajomości języka polskiego następnym pokoleniom.

Nie sposób wymienić wszystkich nazwisk miejscowych polskich patriotów. Jeden z nich, pan Edward Cios, przekazał znaczny spadek na zakup obecnego Domu Parafialnego. Wielu innych latami oddawało swój własny czas i wysiłek na wyremontowanie i utrzymanie domu, który stał się mieszkaniem polskiego ksiedza, centrum wielu spotkań Polaków, a także siedzibą Polskiej Szkoły Sobotniej.

Dzieki temu Msze Święte od czasów obozów demobilizacyjnych odbywająsię w jezyku polskim, a dzieci z rodzin polskich mają możliwość uczęszczania na lekcje religii, przyjęcia Sakramentu Chrztu Świętego, przystąpienia do 1-szej Komunii Świętej, Bierzmowania, a potem Sakramentu Małżeństwa. Na terenie parafii odbywają się także pogrzeby w języku polskim.

Polskiej Szkole Sobotniej w Milford nadano imię Tadeusza Czuchnickiego, mieszkańca obozu demobilizacyjnego Wojska Polskiego na tutejszym terenie. Był on wielkim patriotą, wieloletnim, bezinteresownym działaczem i prezesem Parafii w Milford oraz Kola SPK Nr 107 na tym terenie. Funkcje te sprawował aż do momentu nagłej śmierci w 1993 roku.

Pan Tadeusz brał aktywny udział w życiu szkoły jako prezes i opiekun z ramienia Koła SPK. Niezmęczony organizator wielu imprez patriotycznych na tym terenie jak Obchody Rocznicy Konstytucji 3-go Maja, Świętego Mikołaja, Opłatka Parafialnego, Jajka Wielkanocnego, itp. Był tez autorem wielu wierszy, ktore często były recytowane podczas różnych uroczystości. Panu Tadeuszowi zawdzięczamy istnienie obecnej szkoły, dla ktorej był zawsze wielką podporą moralną i niezastąpioną pomocą.

Obecna kadra nauczycielska pracuje równie ciężko i bezinteresownie kontynuując nauczanie języka polskiego wsród nowego pokolenia Polaków. Dzięki istnieniu Polskiej Szkoły Sobotniej, młodzież ma mozliwość przygotowania się i zdawania egzaminów z języka polskiego jako języka obcego na poziomie małej matury czyli tzw. GCSE, oraz dużej matury AS-A2, uznawanej przez władze szkolne w Anglii, co daje uczniom lepszy start życiowy ze względu na posiadanie dodatkowych punktów, które często okazują się pomocne przy wyborze kierunku studiów.

Szkoła współpracuje ściśle z Polską Macierzą Szkolną w Londynie, która ustala program nauczania i wspomaga szkoły sobotnie oferując programy szkoleniowe dla nauczycieli.

Pierwszymi nauczycielkami w naszej szkole były pani mgr Grażyna Cheshire, dr mgr Zofia Łuklinska, Śp. Księżniczka Natalia Czartoryska, Beata Piwowarek (do 2007) oraz dr Iza Wilczyńska, która obecnie piastuje funkcję skarbnika szkoły.

Inni długoletni nauczyciele szkoły sobotniej w Milford to: mgr Antonina Machowska, mgr Renata Hollebone, mgr Ewa Andrzejewska (do 2008 roku), mgr Izabella Miklas-Sikora, mgr Joanna Krzysztoń, dr mgr Krzysztof Kucharski (do 2009 roku), Zofia Wilczyńska, Renata Pater-Kozłowska oraz mgr Katarzyna Wołyńska.

Prezesem szkoły od dłuższego czasu jest dr mgr Wojciech Machowski. Funkcję dyrektora szkoły nieprzerwanie od 1987 roku pełni dr mgr Zofia Łuklińska.

Mr Edward Cios, whose bequest made it possible to buy the present parish house. Many other parishioners gave their time and effort freely over the years to decorate and maintain the building. As well as the house being the parish priest's home, it also serves as the base for our Polish Saturday morning School.

Masses continue to be celebrated in Polish and thanks to the existence of the school, children of Polish families have the opportunity to attend RE lessons, receive the Sacrament of Baptism, prepare for first Holy Communion, Confirmation and later for marriage. The parish also holds funerals in the Polish language.

The Milford Polish School is named in honour of Tadeusz Czuchnicki, who lived in one of the resettlement camps for Polish Forces in the vicinity. He was very patriotic and worked for the parish voluntarily for many years. He was also a founding member of the Milford 107 Polish Ex-Combatants Association. He was an active member until his sudden death in 1993.

Mr Tadeusz was an active participant in the life of the school and fulfilled the role of President, as well as being a staunch supporter of the Ex-Combatants Association. He worked tirelessly, organising events such as festivities for the Commemoration of the 3 May, St Nicholas' Feast Day and Easter egg hunts. He also wrote poems for many of the Polish parish occasions. We are grateful to him for the founding of the school and for his immense contribution and moral support.

The present school staff is also working hard, on a voluntary basis, for the continued education of the latest generation of children. Thanks to the existence of the Polish Saturday morning school the pupils have the chance to prepare for GCSE, AS and A2 in Polish and foreign languages. This work improves the life chances of our children.

The school works closely with the Polish School Foundation in London which sets the curriculum.

The first teachers of the school were Grażyna Cheshire MA, Dr Zofia Łuklińska, the late Princess Natalia Czartoryska, Beata Piwowarek(until 2007) and Dr Iza Wilczyńska, who is presently our bursar.

Other long serving members of our staff include Antonina Machowska MA, Renata Hollebone MA, Ewa Andrzejewska MA (until 2008), Izabella Miklas-Sikora MA, Joanna Krzysztoń MA, Dr. Krzysztof Kucharski (until 2009) Zofia Wilczyńska, Renata Pater-Kozłowska and Katarzyna Wołyńska MA.

The long serving school's President is Dr Wojciech Machowski. Dr Zofia Łuklińska has been the school's Principal since 1987.

Wybór zdjęć z historii Polskiej Szkoły Sobotniej

Selected photographs, illustrating events at the Saturday morning Polish school

Rok 1996
Nauczycielki-od prawej: Grażyna Cheshire, Śp. Księżniczka Natalia Czartoryska, Zofia Łuklińska, Beata Piwowarek, (z tyłu koleżanka)

1996
Teachers, right to left: Grażyna Cheshire, Princess Natalia Czartoryska, Zofia Łuklińska, Beata Piwowarek, back row: guest

Rok 2003
Rozdanie świadectw

2003
Presentation of Certificates

Rok 1989
Milford Village Hall Przedstawienie z okazji Bożego Narodzenia

1989
Christmas performance at Milford Village Hall

Rok 2008
Spotkanie towarzyskie grona pedagogicznego. Od lewej: Grażyna Cheshire, Kasia Wołyńska, Antonina Machowska, Renata Hollebone, Zofia Łuklińska

2008
Informal staff meeting
From left: Grażyna Cheshire, Kasia Wołyńska, Antonina Machowska, Renata Hollebone, Zofia Łuklińska

Rok 2008
Nauczycielki Renata Pater–Kozłowska (po prawej) oraz Beata Piwowarek z klasą początkująca

2008
Teachers Renata Pater-Kozłowska and Beata Piwowarek with beginners' class

Rok 2009
Zakończenie roku szkolnego.

2009
End of school year

Rok 2011
Wręczenie świadectw

2011
Presentation of certificates

Rok 2008
Występ uczniów pod przewodnictwem Renaty Hollebone – zakończenie roku szkolnego

2008
End of year performance under the guidance of teacher Renata Hollebone

Rok 2011
Przedstawienie na rozpoczęciu roku szkolnego

2011
Performance at the start of the school year

Polscy bohaterowie, którzy żyją wśród nas

autorzy tekstu: Zofia Łuklińska i Marek Plaskota

zdjęcia: Marek Plaskota

Uczniowie Polskiej Szkoły Sobotniej w Milford interesują się genezą naszego ośrodka polskiego w Milford, Surrey, będącego częścią Polskiej Parafii Ave Maria. Utrzymują oni kontakt z żyjącymi nadal byłymi żołnierzami Wojska Polskiego - uczestnikami II Wojny Światowej, którzy mieszkają w okolicach Milford.

W latach 60-tych, po demobilizacji wojsk polskich i rozwiązaniu obozów wojskowych około 120 rodzin, byłych polskich żołnierzy którzy brali udział w 2-giej Wojnie światowej mieszkało w okolicach Godalming, Guildford, Surrey. To właśnie im zawdzięczamy piękny polski sztandar Stowarzyszenia Polskich Kombatantów, koła SPK Nr 107, który znalazł miejsce w polskim domu parafialnym w Milford. Sztandar ten został ufundowany przez członków Koła SPK Nr 107 w Surrey pod przewodnictwem Śp. pana Tadeusza Czuchnickiego zrzeszonych wokół naszej polskiej parafii. Używany jest w czasie obchodów świąt narodowych i religijnych. Uszyty został przez śp. panią Józefę Rakowicz oraz ręcznie wyhaftowany przez członkinie parafii Ave Maria.

Nad tym symbolem Polaków osiedlonych na tych terenach po II Wojnie Światowej opiekę przejęło nowe pokolenie parafian pod egidą obecnego Księdza Proboszcza Mirosława Sławickiego.

Niestety, z biegiem czasu pokolenie wojenne nieubłagalnie przechodzi do historii.

Polish heroes who live amongst us

Auhtors: Zofia Łuklińska and Marek Plaskota

Photographs: Marek Plaskota

The image on the opposite page is that of the 107 Ex-Polish Combatants Association standard.

Pupils from the Saturday morning Polish School in Milford are very interested in the origins of the Polish Centre, which is part of the Ave Maria Parish, Milford in Surrey, and continue to maintain contact with the former World War II Polish servicemen still living in the area.

After the closure of the Polish resettlement camps in the Guildford and Godalming areas by the 1960s, approximately 120 Polish ex- servicemen and their families decided to settle locally. We thank them for the exquisite standard of the 107 Polish Ex-Combatants Association.

The standard, which was funded by members of the Association under the leadership of the late Tadeusz Czuchnicki, now has a home in the Polish Parish Centre and takes pride of place whenever the parish celebrates national and religious festivals. It was sewn by the late Mrs Józefa Rakowicz and hand embroidered by members of the Ave Maria Parish.

The care of this symbolic flag of the post war veterans who settled here has been gratefully undertaken by the new generation of the parish, with the help of the current parish priest, Fr. Mirosław Sławicki.

Inevitably, with time, the wartime generation is passing into history.

Poniższe zdjęcia pochodzą z wizyty naszych uczniów - braci Piotra i Dominica Plaskotów (Członków organizacji Sea Cadets w Guildford) w listopadzie 2011 roku u pana Władysława Adamka, polskiego patrioty, zasłużonego parafianina oraz uczestnika II Wojny Światowej nagrodzonego wieloma medalami za zasługi wojenne przez rządy Polski, Wielkiej Brytanii oraz Holandii. Pan Władysław mieszka od wielu lat w Elstead, Surrey.

These three photographs were taken when two brothers from the Polish Saturday morning School, Piotr and Dominic Plaskota (who are also members of the Sea Cadets in Guildford), visited Mr Władisław Adamek in November 2011. A patriotic Polish veteran and an active member of the parish, Mr Adamek has been honoured by receiving many Polish, British and Dutch military medals, and has lived in Elstead for many years.

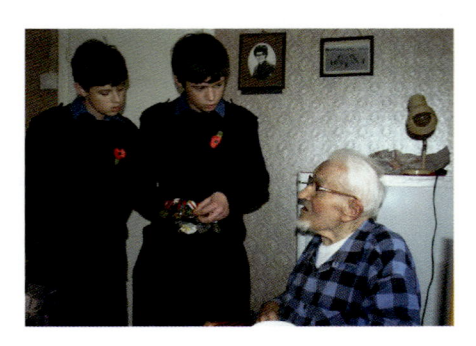

Kolejne dwa zdjęcia zostały zrobione podczas wizyty pana Wilhelma Jokiela uczestnnika II Wojny Światowej w naszej Szkole w listopadzie 2011 roku. Wszyscy uczniowie i nauczyciele wysłuchali z ogromnym zainteresowaniem historii pana Wilhelma, mieszkańca Witley o jego niezwykle niebezpiecznych przeżyciach wojennych oraz losów jego rodziny. Pan Wilhem odpowiedział także na wiele pytań związanych z tym okresem jego życia.

The two photographs on this page were taken in November 2011, when Wilhelm Jokiela, a Polish WWII veteran and a resident of Witley village in Surrey, visited the Polish School. Staff and pupils alike listened with great interest to Mr Jokiela's account of his perilous war time experiences and the fate of his family. Mr Jokiela went on to answer many questions associated with that period of his life.

It was an extremely interesting, moving and, at the same time, an educational experience for the pupils of our school. The visit ended with a viewing of Mr Jokiela's WW II photographs.

Było to bardzo ciekawe i jednocześnie edukacyjne spotkanie dla uczniów naszej szkoły. Wizyta zakończyła sie oglądaniem fotografii z czasów II Wojny Światowej, które pan Wilhem przyniósł ze sobą do szkoły.

Serdecznie dziękujemy naszym bohaterom!

A heartfelt thank you to our heroes!

Nie zapommnijmy o zasiugach tych, ktorzy odeszli

autorzy tekstu: Zofia Łuklińska i Marek Plaskota

zdjęcia: Marek Plaskota

Co roku nasza Polska Szkola Sobotnia w Milford, Surrey łącznie z Polską Parafią uroczyście obchodzi Dzień Wszystkich Świętych, który przypada w Polsce 1-go listopada.

Złożone kwiaty i płonące na grobach polskich żołnierzy znicze są wyrazem hołdu oddanego przez uczniów i nauczycieli Polskiej Szkoły Sobotniej im. Tadeusza Czuchnickiego oraz innych członków Polskiej Parafii w Milford.

Ksiądz Proboszcz Mirosław Sławicki niestrudzenie odwiedza cmentarze w Brookwood, Milford, Elstead, Witley, Godalming, Haslemere, Farnham i Guildford gdzie spoczywają nasi rodacy. Ofiarowywana corocznie modlitwa za zmarłych i poświęcenie mogił są także wyrazem hołdu oddanego tym, którzy walczyli o naszą wolność. Jest to także czas zadumy i refleksji.

Główne uroczystości obchodzimy na cmentarzu wojskowym w Brookwood koło Woking. Polski Cmentarz wojskowy w Brookwood został utworzony po II Wojnie Światowej w celu upamiętnienia żołnierzy Wojska Polskiego którzy polegli w walce z hitlerowskim najeźćcą i są pochowani na licznych cmentarzach na terenie Wielkiej Brytanii.

Lest we forget

Text: Zofia Łuklińska and Marek Plaskota

Photographs: Marek Plaskota

Every year our Saturday morning Polish School joins with the parish to celebrate All Saints' Day on 1 November.

Pupils and teachers from the school pay their respects to the Polish ex-servicemen, in the name of all the parishioners, by placing flowers and candles on their graves.

As part of the holy day our parish priest Fr. Sławicki, visits cemeteries at Brookwood, Milford, Elstead, Witley, Godalming, Haslemere, Farnham and Guildford where Polish soldiers are buried. The prayers and blessing of graves are also symbols of honour for the fallen Polish soldiers, who gave their lives for our freedom. It is also a time for quiet contemplation.

The main ceremony takes place at the Polish Military section of Brookwood Cemetery near Woking. This was established after the Second World War in remembrance of the members of the Polish Forces who died fighting alongside the Allies against Hitler and for those who are buried in numerous cemeteries in Great Britain.

W tym dniu nad główną kwaterą poległych żołnierzy polskich, nieopodal pięknego pomnika autorstwa słynnego polskiego artysty prof. Bronisława Chromego, ufundowanego przez Ambasadę Polską w Londynie, powiewa wysoko polska biało-czerwona flaga.

Pod tym pomnikiem, każdego roku parafianie składają symboliczne biało-czerwone kwiaty i zapalają znicze. Po ofiarowanej modlitwie cała procesja przechodzi do położonej nieco dalej kwatery polskich marynarzy, aby im rowniez oddac cześć i hołd.

Na cmentarzu w Brookwood jest rownież wiele grobów naszych parafian. Groby te są skupionych głównie w okolicy pomnika z orłem.

Napisy na grobach, często zawierają informację o miejscu urodzenia w Polsce, pobycie na wygnaniu w Rosji, uczestnictwie w ostatniej wojnie w szeregach armii Gen. Władysława Andersa czy wojsk alianckich.

Wszyscy Oni przyczynili sie do tego, że możemy żyć, cieszyć się wolnością i swobodnie podróżować po Europie i świecie. Niestety, wielu z nich jednak osobiście nie doczekalo już tego momentu.

Listopad jest również miesiącem w którym starsi uczniowie Polskiej Szkoły Sobotniej w Milford odwiedzają groby tych, którzy przyczynili się do utworzenia i byli zaangażowani w prowadzenie tej szkoły. Na cmentarzu w Godalming spoczywa patron szkoły - Tadeusz Czuchnicki.

Do grona tych osób należała także jedna z nauczycielek szkoły - Księżniczka Natalia Maria Gabriela Czartoryska herbu Pogoń Litewska, której prochy spoczywają na cmentarzu w Milford.

Cześć ich pamięci

164

On this day the red and white flag of Poland flies high above the graves of fallen Polish soldiers, near the beautiful memorial designed by the famous Polish artist Professor Bronislaw Chromy and donated by the Polish Embassy in London.

Every year our parishioners offer prayers, light candles and place red and white flowers at the foot of the memorial. Afterwards the procession makes its way to the Polish Naval section at the cemetery to pay tribute to the Polish sailors who died in WWII.

Many headstones of the interred soldiers' graves carry inscriptions about their place of birth in Poland, deportation to the Soviet Union, and participation in the Second World War as an allied army under the command of General Władyslaw Anders.

Their contribution has given us liberty and the chance to travel freely around Europe and the rest of the world. Unfortunately, many of them did not survive to see this moment.

Many other people of our parish are also buried at Brookwood Cemetery, mainly near the statue of the eagle.

November is also the month in which the older pupils visit the graves of our patron Tadeusz Czuchnicki, who is buried in Godalming cemetery, and Princess Natalia Maria Gabriela Czartoryska, who was one of the teachers at the school and whose ashes are interred at Milford Cemetery. Both of them were instrumental in establishing the Saturday morning Polish School at Milford.

We honour their memory

By their own hand

Selected examples of work completed by pupils from Saturday morning Polish School at Milford

Emigracja moich Rodziców

Marek Płaskota i Marzena Wiśniewska pobrali się w Polsce, w Waśnowie. Tata się trochę nauczył Angielskiego przed przyjazdem do Anglii, ale Mama nie znała tego języka. W Polsce w tamtych czasach prace nie były dobrze płatne, bo ekonomia kraju była niska po wojnie. Było dosyć dużo prac, bo populacja kraju się zmniejszyła, ale zarobki były niskie. To już było długo po wojnie, ale efekty nadal były, i są nadal w Polsce. Tata z Mamą zdecydowali się przenieść do Anglii na jakiś czas i zobaczyć czy lepsze prace. Po jakimś czasie Tata dostał pracę jako pielęgniarz, a Mama również trochę później. Potem ja i Dominic urodziliśmy się, więc Mama i Tata zdecydowali zostać w Anglii.

Po piętnastu latach w Anglii moi rodzice są zadowoleni z pobytu, bo ich plany zostały spełnione. Ja również uważam, że decyzja moich rodziców była dobra, bo ja i mój brat umiemy mówić i pisać po polsku i po angielsku. Razem z bratem chodzimy do Polskiej Szkoły Sobotniej, Milford, Surrey, która jest bardzo blisko mojego domu.

Piotr Płaskota, 28 Styczeń 2012
Lat: 14

The Emigration of Polish People to England

Marek Plaskota and Marzena Wiśniewska got married in a little town called Waśniów in Poland. My Dad (Marek) had learnt English before his emigration to England. However my Mum (Marzena) had not learnt this language; she had to learn it herself in England. At the time the jobs in Poland weren't well paid because the economy was low, as Poland was still recovering after the war (although it was still long after the war). Even though it had been several decades after the war, (1990's) the population of Poland had still decreased; leaving several jobs available. However, a lot of these jobs had low wages. My Mum and Dad decided to emigrate to England in search of better jobs, despite the fact my Mum didn't know English. After some time, both my Mum and Dad became nurses, however my Mum became a nurse later. Later on me and my brother Dominic were born and then my parents decided to stay in England.

My parents after 15 years in England are happy with their choice, because their plans were fulfilled. I also think that my parents choice was good, because I now know two languages fluently, however I still learn Polish in school on Saturday. I attend Polish School in Milford, Surrey, which is very close to my house.

Piotr Plaskota   28th January 2012
Age: 14

28/1/12

<u>Emigracja Polaków</u>

Moi rodzice przenieśli się tutaj do Anglii, bo tutaj jest więcej szans na lepszą pracę i też dla nas (mnie i mego brata) jest łatwiej się uczyć. Ja uczę się dobrze przez to, że tutaj mieszkamy blisko mojej szkoły, i przez to nie musimy płacić za benzynę, aby dojechać do szkoły, tylko mogę używać szkolny autobus. Mój brat Piotrek chodzi ze mną do tej samej szkoły, ale on jest o prawie dwa lata starszy ode mnie, to znaczy, że chodzi do starszej klasy. Moi rodzice pracują jako pielęgniarze w szpitalu. Obydwoje pochodzą z Polski i też bardzo blisko siebie mieszkali. Mój tata pochodzi z Ostrowca Świętokrzyskiego a mama z Grzegorzowic.

Moi rodzice, po piętnastu latach w Anglii są bardzo zadowoleni z pobytu tutaj przez to, że ich plany zostały spełnione. Ja również uważam, że decyzja moich rodziców była właściwa.

Przez ostatnie sześć lat chodzę do Polskiej Szkoły Sobotniej w Milford, Surrey, gdzie nauczyłem się czytać i pisać po polsku. Jestem z tego bardzo zadowolony, bo podczas wyjazdów do Polski mogę porozumiewać się z babcią i dziadkiem oraz nawiązywać znajomości z nowymi kolegami. Nasza szkoła naucza nas również historii naszego narodu oraz polskiej kultury i tradycji. Z projektu o obozach demobilizacyjnych w Anglii, dowiedzieliśmy się, że taka sama szkoła istniała zaraz po drugiej wojnie światowej w hrabstwie Surrey.

Dominic Płaskota, 12 lat.

28/1/12

Polish Emigration

My parents emigrated to England, because there is more occasions for better jobs and it is better for us (me and my brother) because we live close to my school. I learn well, and that is because we don't have to pay for petrol, to get to school, I can just take the school bus. My brother Piotrek goes to the same school as me, but he is nearly two years older than me, so he is in an older class. My parents are both nurses, and both Polish, when they lived in Poland they lived very close to each other, my dad in Ostrowiec Świętokrzyski and my mum from Ozdzoszowice.

My parents, after 15 years in England are very glad that they made the right decision, to Emigrate. I too think that their decision was right.

For the last 6 years I go to the Polish Saturday School in Milford, Surrey, where I learnt to read and write in polish. I am very happy that I go to this school, for when we go on holiday I can talk to my Grandma and Grandpa, also I can make new friends. My school also teaches me about Polish history, culture and traditions. From the project about demobilisation camps I learnt that my school was still there right after the World War.

Dominic Płachota   Polish Saturday School   12 lat

14 Styczeń 2012

Emigracja mojej rodziny do Anglii

Moja Mama przyjechała do Anglii w Maju roku 2005, ja mieszkałem z babcią i dziadkiem w Polsce. We Wrześniu roku 2006 przyjechałem do Anglii, zacząłem szkołę cztery dni po przyjechaniu do Anglii.
Przyjechała moja mama ze względu na brak pracy w naszym mieście. Nasze miasto jest bardzo ciche i nic się nie miało zmienić. Mama zawsze chciała mieszkać zawsze za granicą i to była najlepsza szansa.
Ogólnie my się nazywamy ekonomicznymi emigrantami i jesteśmi bardzo zadowoleni z życia tu w Anglii.

14th January 2012

The imigration of my family to England

My mother imigrated to England in the May of 2005, whilst I lived in Poland with my Grandad and Grandma. In Poland. In the very late August of 2006 I came over to England, and I started school 4 days after arriving in the United Kingdom.
There was a lack of Employment in my town and very Little opportunity for the future. My Mother therefore decided to come to England to give us a better start in life here in England
Overall, we are very impressed by the way our life has turned out here. We would call ourselves econonmical Imigrants and are really happy with our lives in England.

Mikołaj Marciniak, Saturday School in Milgard

Dzieci w czasie II wojny światowej nie miały zabawek ze sklepów. One musiały robić swoje własne zabawki. Wszystkie gry i zabawy musiały wymyślać. Ponieważ nie było puzli, gier planszowych, itp. Z babci opowiadań dowiedziałam się że jedną z ich ulubionych gier było kółko i krzyżyk. Nie było komputerów ani gier. I gry play station, DSI, i takie gry. Dlatego dzieci spędzały więcej czasu z koleżankami, kolegami i rodziną.

Children could not buy toys or games during the Second World War. They had to make their own.

From what my grandmother told me, one of the favourite games was noughts and crosses. There were no computers, play stations, DSI, or other such games. This is why children spent more time with friends and parents.

Agata Kuciaba, age 6

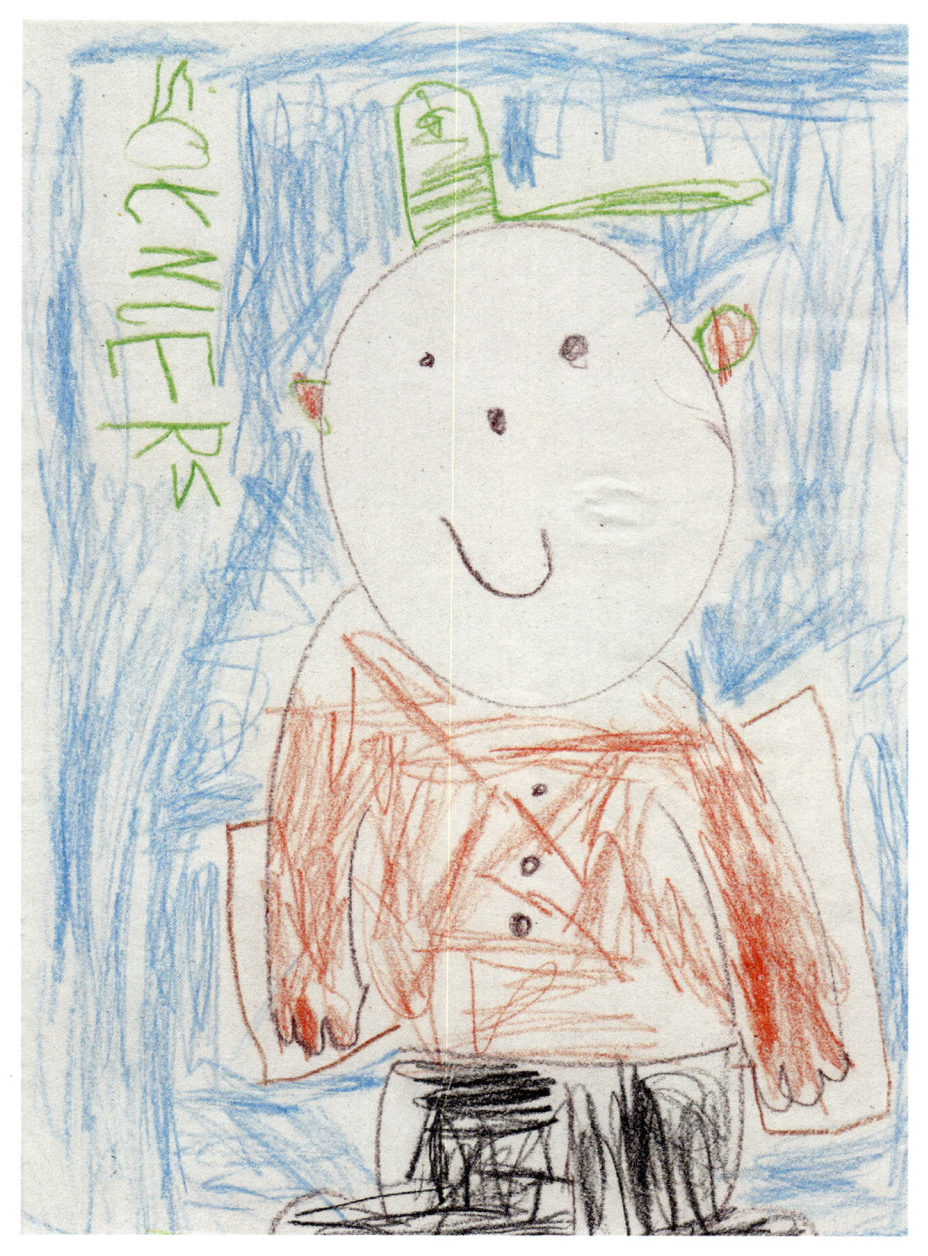

Adam Wiśniowski, age 5

Mój Dziadek

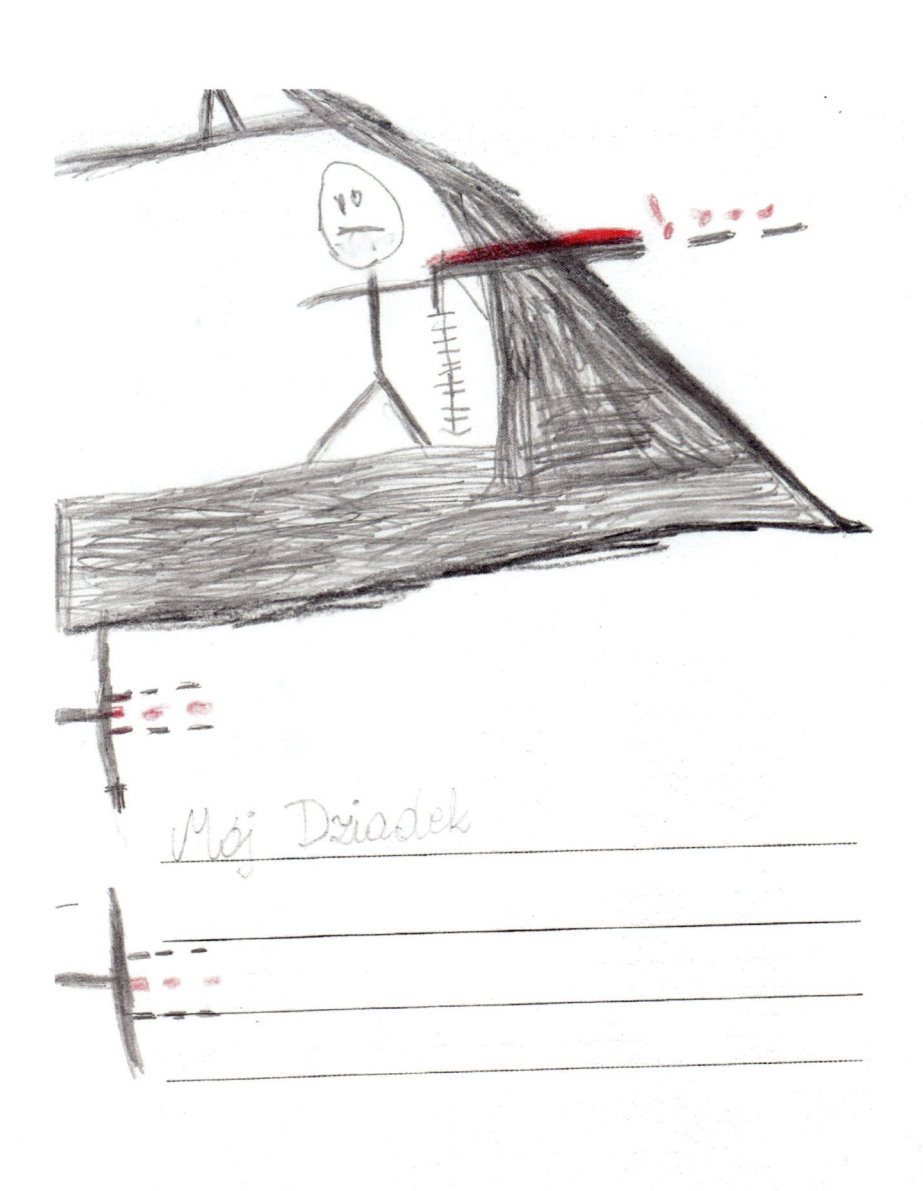

My Grand-dad - Tomek Cowley, age 6

War - Kuba Szumiański, age 8

Bartek Szumlański, age 6

Our History - Mikołaj Marciniak, age 12

Grand Opening

26th August 2012

Piotr Plaskota, age 14

Image credits

Chapter 1
p. 12	-	Top image	©	Zen Rogalski
	-	Fig. 1:1	©	History of Thursley Society
p.13	-	Fig. 1:2	©	National Archives (NA) (Kew) with permission to annotate
p.14	-	Fig. 1:3	©	Zen Rogalski
p.15	-	Fig. 1:4 and Fig. 1:5	©	Zen Rogalski
p.16	-	Fig. 1:6 and Fig. 1:7	©	Zen Rogalski
p.17	-	Fig.1 :8	©	Private collection of Sergeant (Retired) Bernard (Bern) Keegan
	-	Annotated photograph	©	Zen Rogalski
	-	Fig. 1:9	©	Zen Rogalski
p.18	-	Fig. 1:10 and Fig. 1:11	©	Zen Rogalski
p.19	-	Fig. 1:12 and Fig. 1:13	©	Zen Rogalski
p.20	-	Portion of photograph	©	Portion of Photograph, B Modzelan private collection, courtesy of I Modzelan
	-	Fig. 1:14	©	Zen Rogalski
p.21	-	Fig. 1:15	©	English Heritage

Chapter 2
p.22	-	Top image	©	Zen Rogalski
p.23	-	Fig. 2:1	©	Portion of photograph from Lorne Scots Museum, Canada
p.24	-	Fig. 2:2	©	Lorne Scots Museum, Canada
p.26	-	Fig. 2:3	©	Zen Rogalski
	-	Fig. 2:4	©	Zen Rogalski
p.27	-	Fig. 2:5	©	Zen Rogalski
	-	Fig. 2:6	©	Zen Rogalski
p.28	-	Fig. 2:7 and Fig. 2:8	©	Private collection of Sergeant (Retired) Bernard (Bern) Keegan
p.29	-	Figs. 2:9 to 2:12	©	Private collection of Sergeant (Retired) Bernard (Bern) Keegan

Chapter 3
p.30	-	Top image	©	Zen Rogalski
p.31	-	Fig. 3:1	©	US Military. Under the terms of Title 17, Chapter 1, Section 105 of the US Code
		Fig.3 :2	©	This work is excerpted from an official document of the United Nations. The policy of this organisation is to keep most of its documents in the public domain in order to disseminate "as widely as possible the ideas (contained) in the United Nations Publications", (retrieved 4 April 2012)
p.32	-	Fig. 3:3	©	Zen Rogalski
p.33	-	Fig. 3:4	©	This image is in the public domain according to Article 4, case 2 of the Polish Copyright Law Act of February 4, 1994 (Dz. U. z 2006r. Nr 90 poz. 631) with later changes
p.34	-	Graphics and text	©	Zen Rogalski
p.35	-	Graphics and text	©	Zen Rogalski
p.36	-	Graphics and text	©	Zen Rogalski
p.37	-	Graphics and text	©	Zen Rogalski
p.38	-	Graphics and text	©	Zen Rogalski
p.39	-	Graphics and text	©	Zen Rogalski

Chapter 4
p.40	-	Top image	©	Zen Rogalski
		Fig. 4:1	©	Zen Rogalski
p.41	-	Fig. 4:2	©	Zen Rogalski
p.46	-	Fig. 4:3	©	Zen Rogalski
p.47	-	Fig. 4:4 to 4:7	©	Benon Tuszyński private coillection

Chapter 5
p.48	-	Top image	©	Zen Rogalski
p.49	-	Fig. 5:1	©	Zen Rogalski
p.50 -51	-	Graphics and text	©	Zen Rogalski
	-	All photograph portions	©	B Modzelan private collection, courtesy of I Modzelan

Chapter 6
| p.52 | - | Top image | © | Zen Rogalski |

178

p.53	-	Fig. 6:1	©	Canadian War Museum
p.54	-	Fig. 6:2	©	Zen Rogalski
	-	Fig. 6:3	©	Document portions from the Polish Institute and Sikorski Museum (PISM)
p.55	-	Fig. 6:4	©	Janina Lis private collection
	-	Fig. 6:5	©	Zen Rogalski
p.57	-	Fig. 6:6	©	Portion of WO document, NA
p.59	-	Fig. 6:7	©	From documents at the PISM

Chapter 7

p.60	-	Top image	©	Zen Rogalski
	-	Fig. 7:1	©	Portion of photograph, English Heritage
p.61	-	Fig. 7:2	©	Wies and Zen Rogalski private collection
	-	Fig. 7:3	©	Primus stove : this work has been released into the public domain by its author, John Fogarty at the English Wikipedia project; other images Zen Rogalski; arrangement Zen Rogalski
p.62	-	Fig. 7:4	©	Zen Rogalski
p.62	-	Fig. 7:5	©	Zen Rogalski; artefact held by the Rural Life Centre (RLC)
p.63	-	Fig. 7:6 and 7:7	©	Zen Rogalski; artefacts held by RLC
p.64	-	Fig. 7:8	©	Stanisława Sysiak private collection
	-	Fig. 7:9	©	Zen Rogalski
p.65	-	Fig. 7:10	©	Władysław and Waldue Adamek, and Maggie Lee (née Adamek) private collection
	-	Fig. 7:11	©	Zen Rogalski
p.66	-	Fig. 7:12	©	Zen Rogalski; artefacts held by the RLC
p.67	-	Fig. 7:13	©	Zen Rogalski; artefacts held by the RLC
	-	Fig. 7:14	©	Applied for

Chapter 8

p.68	-	Top image	©	Zen Rogalski
p.69	-	Fig. 8:1		Portion of Photograph, B Modzelan private collection, courtesy of I Modzelan
	-	Figs. 8:2 and 8:3	©	Wies and Zen Rogalski private collection
p.70	-	Figs. 8:4 and 8:5	©	Wies and Zen Rogalski private collection
p.71	-	Fig. 8:6	©	Wies and Zen Rogalski private collection
	-	Fig. 8:7	©	I Modzelan private collection, contributed to the *Tweedsmuir Camp Exhibition*; Wies and Zen Rogalski private collection; images: Zen Rogalski
p.72	-	Figs. 8:8 and 8:9	©	Wies and Zen Rogalski private collection
p.73	-	Figs. 8:10 and 8:11	©	Zen Rogalski
p.74	-	Fig. 8:12	©	Dymitr Czertko and family private collection
p.74	-	Fig. 8:13	©	Secretts
p.75	-	Fig. 8:14	©	Barbara Januszewska's private collection

Chapter 9

p.76	-	Top image	©	Zen Rogalski
p.77	-	Fig.9:1	©	Maggie Lee (née Adamek) private collection
	-	Fig. 9:2	©	Irene Modzelan private collection
p.78	-	Fig. 9:3	©	Stanisława Sysiak private collection
	-	Fig. 9:4	©	Wies and Zen Rogalski private collection; Dymitr Czertko and family private collection
p.79	-	Fig. 9:5	©	B Modzelan private collection, courtesy of I Modzelan
	-	Figs. 9:6 and 9:7	©	Wies and Zen Rogalski private collection
p.80	-	Fig. 9:8	©	Arrangement Zen Rogalski
	-	Fig. 9:9	©	Applied for
p.81	-	Fig. 9:10	©	Stanisława Sysiak private collection; Wies and Zen Rogalski private collection

Chapter 10

p.82	-	Top image	©	Zen Rogalski
p.83	-	Fig. 10:1	©	National Archives and Records Administration (NARA), USA
	-	Fig. 10:2	©	Krystyna Łazarczyk private collection
p.84	-	Fig. 10:3	©	George Jopek private collection
	-	Fig. 10:4	©	Zen Rogalski
p.85	-	Fig. 10:5	©	Portion of photograph, Wies and Zen Rogalski private collection
	-	Fig. 10:6	©	Artefact held by the Victoria and Albert Museum of Childhood
p.86	-	Fig. 10:7	©	Portion of certificate, from I Modzelan private collection
p.87	-	Fig. 10.8	©	Certificate, from I Modzelan private collection
p.88	-	Fig. 10:9	©	Zen Rogalski

p.89	-	Fig. 10:10	© Wies and Zen Rogalski private collection
p.90	-	Fig. 10:11	© Artefacts held by the Victoria and Albert Museum of Childhood
p.91	-	Fig. 10:12	© Portion of photograph George Jopek private collection, Wies and Zen Rogalski private collection, Stanisława Sysiak private collection

Chapter 11

p.92	-	Top image	© Zen Rogalski
p.96	-	Fig. 11:1	© Stanisława Sysiak private collection
p.98	-	Fig.11:2	© Zen and Wies Rogalski private collection, B Modzelan private collection, courtesy of I Modzelan
p.99-101	-	All images	© Zen Rogalski

Chapter 12

p.102	-	Top image	© Zen Rogalski
	-	Fig. 12:1	© Zen Rogalski
p.103	-	Fig. 12:2	© Dymitr Czertko and family private collection
	-	Fig. 12:3	© George Jopek private collection
p.104	-	Fig. 12:4	© Dymitr Czertko and family private collection
p.105	-	Fig, 12:5	© Zen Rogalski
p.106	-	All images	© Zen Rogalski
p.107	-	Fig. 12:9	© Wies Rogalski private collection
	-	Fig. 12.10	© Wies Rogalski
p.108-109	-	All images	© Zen Rogalski
p.110	-	Fig. 12:14	© Zen Rogalski
p.111	-	Fig. 12:15	© Wies and Zen Rogalski private collection

Chapter 13

p.112	-	Top image	© Zen Rogalski
	-	Fig. 13:1	© Waldue Adamek
p.113	-	Fig. 13.2	© File:15-alongside in Thorshavn Faroes April1970.jpg, Wikipedia, free: to share – to copy, distribute and transmit the work, to remix – to adapt the work (retrieved 6 April 2012)
	-	Fig. 13.3	© 'Apcbg', in the public domain, Wikipedia, (retrieved 10 October 2010)
p.114	-	Fig. 13:4	© Edward Burczy private collection
p.116	-	Fig. 13:5	© Edward Burczy private collection
p.117	-	Fishing scene	© Zen Rogalski
p.118	-	Fig.13:6	© Elizabeth Hopkins (née Zimna) private collection
	-	Fig. 13:7	© Elizabeth Hopkins (née Zimna) private collection
p.120	-	Figs. 13:8 and 13.9	© Mike Kot private collection
p.121	-	Figs. 13:10 and 13.11	© Mike Kot private collection
p.122	-	Fig. 13:12	© Mike Kot private collection
	-	Fig. 13:13	© Maggie Lee (née Adamek) private collection
p.123	-	Fig. 13:14	© Maggie Lee (née Adamek) private collection
p.124	-	Fig. 13:15	© Maggie Lee (née Adamek) private collection
p.125	-	Fig. 13:16	© Janina Lis private collection
p.127	-	Figs. 13:17and 13:18	© I Modzelan private collection, contributed to the *Tweedsmuir Camp Exhibition*
p.128	-	Fig. 13 19	© Wies Rogalski private collection
p.129	-	Fig. 13.20	© Alex Rogalska
	-	London skyline	© Zen Rogalski
p.130	-	Fig. 13:21	© Zen Rogalski
p.131	-	Fig. 13:22	© Alleyn's School photograph, Zen Rogalski private collection
p.132	-	Fig. 13:23	© Wies and Zen Rogalski private collection
p.134	-	Fig. 13:24	© Wies and Zen Rogalski private collection
p.135	-	Fig. 13:24	© 123people.co.uk

Chapter 14

p.136	-	Top image	© Zen Rogalski
p.142	-	Fig. 14:1	© Original table Ministry of Labour, NA (Kew)
p.149	-	Fig. 14:2	© Released into the public domain by the copyright holder, 'Poeticibent'
p.150	-	Fig. 14:3	© Zen Rogalski

Chapter 15

p.152	-	Top image	© Saturday morning Polish School, Milford
p.156-158	-	All images	© Marek Plaskota
p.159	-	Drawing	© Mikołaj Marciniak
p.160-162	-	All images	© Marek Plaskota
p.164	-	All images	© Marek Plaskota

p.165	-	Drawing	©	Piotr Plaskota
p.172	-	Drawing	©	Agata Kuciaba
p.173	-	Drawing	©	Adam Wiśniowski
p.174	-	Drawing	©	Tomek Cowley
p.175	-	Top drawing	©	Kuba Szumiański
	-	Bottom drawing	©	Bartek Szumiański
p.176	-	Drawing	©	Mikołaj Marciniak
p.177	-	Drawing	©	Piotr Plaskota

Every effort has been made to establish copyright and contact copyright holders prior to publication. If contacted, the publishers will be pleased to rectify any omissions or errors at the earliest opportunity.